Journey into Unknown

JOURNEY INTO UNKNOWN

An Autobiography

KAZA ARJUNARAO

PARTRIDGE

A Penguin Company

ISBN: Softcover   978-1-4828-1351-7
             Ebook   978-1-4828-1350-0

Partridge books may be ordered through booksellers or by contacting:

Partridge India
Penguin Books India Pvt.Ltd
11, Community Centre, Panchsheel Park, New Delhi 110017
India
www.partridgepublishing.com
Phone: 000.800.10062.62

CONTENTS

SYNOPSIS

It has been an endeavor of human being throughout the history of mankind to seek truth and God.

I was perturbed by the in-equalities in creation on earth. Most of the creatures on earth either on land or under water exist by preying on other creatures, including human being. There is yawning gap among human beings themselves either in intelligence or in robustness or in appearance or in communication skills etc. There is also a yawning gap in general in capabilities, particularly physical, between one gender and its opposite gender. In the entire history of creation, it is observed that might prevails over week and meek. Natural disasters strike one part of the world or the other at regular intervals. Diseases are common occurrence. One deadly disease after another strike human beings at regular intervals. When God is omnipotent omniscient, omnipresent and magnanimous to all, why these inequalities and calamities, the explanations of science not withstanding? Several religions have been founded in course of time based on the teachings of saints said to be revelations of God to answer these questions.

Our universe is considered to be continuously expanding the extent of which is at present incomprehensible and as such is infinite and is much as 40 million million million light years. There are billions of stars in the universe. In the above scenario, the magnitude of our planet is infinitely small as to be almost nothing. On such a planet exists a proud creature called human being.

The age of universe is estimated at around 15000 million years and its life is considered to be infinite as per the present estimates.

The sun may be present in the universe with more or less brilliance for another 10000 million years which can be adventurously assumed as the life span of species on our planet. The present average life span of a human being is only 60 years. Considering the infiniteness of the universe in time and space, it is quite puzzling as to which catalyst generates pride in human being.

In my Journey into unknown, I tried to find answers to these unpleasant improprieties as I was not satisfied with preachings of various religions.

My evolution from meekness and naivety to bravery and wisdom as I grew from adolescence to adult hood with exposure to literature of Europe and to society of various hues of people in the university is discussed. But for occasional forays into outside world intended for deserting all materialistic attachments, which were though aborted at nascent stage, I spent most of my time in university brooding over ifs and buts of creation, God and human in solitude.

After marriage till its breakdown, I was fully immersed in my Job and did not give much thought to my ultimate goal. After my second marriage, I started again to meditate on the issue whenever time permitted. During this process, I felt that I had acquired meta physical powers when a thought flashed through my mind. I experimented with the powers to achieve some astounding results. But alas, I fell prey to these powers soon after wards. The consequences were catastrophic and I all most became insane. The travails and trauma almost lasted twenty five years, which however did not affect my profession in any way. My meditation through all these years and my experiments with supernatural powers culminated into certain firm conclusions about Creator, God, religion, society and human.

A stream of life of my times passes through the entire narration.

In the end, I am to state that an honest and sincere attempt has been made to unravel the mysteries in a rational manner as far as possible taking recourse to popular scientific beliefs wherever necessary.

The autobiography is however narrated in third person.

This is an humble presentation form a common man.

CHAPTER 1

1948-1964

The village was scattered along the national highway, about 10km from the town. It was a big village, being the headquarters of a taluk. The soils of the land in and around the village were sandy clay containing high degree of sandy minerals, which were not suitable for cultivation. The only source of sweet drinking water was a big beautiful lake at the edge of the old village in the northern direction as the ground water was salty. At about 4 km from the village, in the northern direction, there were vast uplands suitable for cultivation of dry crops. Below these uplands and nearer to the village there were large tracts of lands of salty soils at a lower elevation not suitable for cultivation. But, there existed a naturally formed huge, bund curving along their extreme edge in east westerly direction resulting in the formation of a huge reservoir with a shallow valley on the other side. The main sources of livelihood for the residents were agricultural activities, the intensity of which generally depends on the vagaries of nature. An aerodrome not in commercial use also existed near the village.

Four brothers in search of cheap agricultural land ultimately landed in this village. They together bought some upland and some lowland and settled in the village. These brothers had little education but were hard working and innovative in their own way. Even though the upland was suitable for commercial crops like tobacco and chilies, they had little holdings of this land. They mainly bought the low land at throwaway prices. There were some pieces of land near the airport at about 2km from the village along the national highway in eastern direction, containing fertile soils up to great depths. They bought the land at a cheap price, as they are lying unused and dug tons and tons of these soils and transported them to their low lands and spread a thick layer of these soils over these lands. They laid their own water distribution system and built pipe sluices through the big bund. Whenever monsoon was normal, the reservoir was filled with water, which was more than sufficient for growing paddy on these prepared lands.

Of the four brothers, the second eldest had taken on lease a house that had been in disuse for several years and which had inadvertently become the residence of bats. He gathered children in the locality to kill the bats during day time and refurbished the house suitable enough to reside.

He, the second eldest brother was bony and thin with a depressed stomach but with strong legs and arms. His wife was a stocky woman with lots of vibrancy and initiative. She was very fond of relatives and treated them very well. They had two daughters. They married off the eldest daughter into a peasant family, whose ancestors were once big landlords residing in a tiny village far away from their place. They married off the younger one to her uncle who by his profession usually resided in Northern provinces. The eldest daughter had two children, one a female and the other a male. Unfortunately, the eldest daughter died of disease that could not be cured, when the male was only two years old. The parents of the diseased woman were very grieved and unfortunately came to the conclusion that their daughter had expired because of the negligence of their son-in-law in getting her timely and proper treatment by a qualified doctor, and this grouse remained ever after. The children were adopted by their material grandparents and thus they came to live with this family in this big village.

The people of the village could generally be classified into three categories or classes. The first category were those who were self-dependent or had enough resources for leading a decent life, who were conglomerate of peasants, business people and educated employees in the government service. The second category were those who could considered to be having no resources or assets of their own and mainly depended on the resources of others to provide them employment to eke out their living, who were conglomerate of several sects considered to be the weaker sections of the society, most of whom had virtually no formal education. The third category, called untouchables, were not allowed to enter into the houses of other classes of the society and even into the temples because of religious dogmatism. These people generally earned their living by making foot wear from raw leather, rearing pigs and doing other odd jobs that none others would not even like to do even in their dreams.

While residential areas of the first category had spacious houses and wide enough roads, the houses of the second category were in close clusters, which were cramped of space with narrow lanes but were generally clean. It is better not to say anything about the residing place of the third category, which was most unhygienic with lots of dirt strewn around and foul smell emitting from all over and were completely isolated from the village. This involuntary un-hygienic sense and their abnormal mental attitude could be simulated in also the so called civilized sane man who could also be transformed into an insane person by perpetual inhuman treatment and complete isolation.

Those were early years of independence. The glitter surrounding national leaders had not yet waned. The national leaders were generally talked about in awe and admiration. Whenever they came down to tour the districts of the area, they alighted at the airport and conducted their tours by car. It was festive occasion for the village folk. All sections of village folk utilized this great opportunity to see their great national leaders in flesh at close quarters, for which special arrangements were usually made at the airport.

Old habits die hard. The behavior of the upper sections of the society towards weaker sections had hardly changed. All kinds of abuses were still hurled upon these people. As everybody knows, this had been happening for centuries. Considering the fact that all classes had people of similar cultural background, and practiced same religion and that they were of the same lineage, this type of discrimination towards majority of their populace was not observed in any other part of the world. This hypothetical division which was tried to be legitimized in the modern era could be actually traced to religious dogmatism in ancient times. This division was such that only certain classes of people were allowed to get educated and that, probably, certain sections of the society who were physically strong were put in charge of agriculture and security and the remaining sections subjugating to them to fulfill their needs. Naturally, this had made higher echelons of the society richer, stronger and more intelligent and conversely made lower echelons physically, mentally and economically weaker. This peculiar trait of human being to subjugate everything in nature including his fellow human beings who were vulnerable, coupled with the absence of a democratic administration for several centuries, must have played a vital role in not allowing the weaker classes from coming out of the morass that had set in. They had become habituated to their way of life and a feeling of resignation had set in so much so that a state of mind which bore no remorse against anybody for their plight had developed. However, the freedom struggle against foreign rule, and subsequently the advent of independence, and a democratic state, had rekindled in them long dead flames of hope of a better future. Leaders from these classes also had begun to emerge under the changed scenario. The desires for better future were silently but strongly creeping into their minds, even though it had not yet led to any degree of belligerence.

The boy was growing in the house of his grandparents in this socio-economic scenario with an inner feeling of pride of being part of the dominant class of the village. The boy was very timid and extremely shy in nature, the extent of which can be gauged from the fact that he would not even look straight into the faces of persons he was talking to even if they were his own gender and then it can be naturally surmised that the question of talking to opposite gender did not arise unless they were his close relatives. He was quite going, honest in his work, and truthful in his talk. He was tall and thin and an awkward boy to look at. He was studious but not hardworking. He was intelligent but naive. He was deeply religious. He not only had the habit of praying to god before going to bed but also had the habit of self-assessment of his deeds during the day. This self assessment, at the later stages of his life, had expanded to critical assessment of his surroundings and the readings he occasionally indulged in, which might ultimately had played an important role in moulding his character as he grew old.

During the period of his secondary education, he developed intimacy with three of his classmates solely because of their initiative and desire to have close rapport with him. These friends were not studious and got through 11th standard after more than one attempt.

One is a stocky well-built boy of average height and of dark complexion but with a charming face of well formed features, and of pleasant manners. He continued his studies and somehow got through the pre-university course. He had an elder sister in town, whose spouse ran a successful road transport company there. They had a very beautiful daughter of very fair complexion and two younger sons. They had married their daughter to this young man and placed him in charge of the transport company after his un-successful attempt at pursuing engineering degree. It seemed that his niece had agreed to marry him after some reluctance. His shrewdness in judging people and an uncanny knack of managing them had helped him in running the company very successfully and in its expansion. In the meantime, his nephews had grown up and began breathing on his neck. He had developed haughtiness that come to some people with success. He also developed a sense of aloofness and a kind of recklessness, most probably arising out of the thought that even though he owed this success to his own efforts he owned nothing and that nobody recognized his efforts the cause of which can be partly traced to his haughtiness and partly to the well laid foundation already excising in the company. The old charm was gone. He had become quite hefty and his face had become fat with flesh. He had become ugly to look at.

The second boy was lean and also of darkish complexion. But his limbs were very agile and flexible. He was very good at yogic exercises and had an artistic flavor. It seemed that he had no family of his own. He lived in the house of the local post master along with an young beautiful girl whom he called his own sister. He was always used to grumble about the miseries that befell on him. But nobody knew the actual truth, as he was used to tell different stories to different people. Otherwise, he was a quiet good natured boy, but somewhat somber. He discontinued his studies after 11th standard and for sometime was engaged in petty odd jobs. He finally settled in a stone slabs depot as engraver of letters on polished stones. Meanwhile, it seemed that he had realized the importance of a good physique and gradually developed a very robust and muscular body. Then, he started collecting street children and gang men of the railways and soon became a leader of a small gang. He had become quite handy to his depot owner as well as to the friend we learnt about previously, to settle the disputes that usually arose from time to time during transactions of their business. He married the daughter of the depot owner, who was ugly to look at and who was averse to do any household chores. He therefore settled in his father-in-law's house. Still, his somberness had not diminished. He was not a happy man, because he had become highly ambitious. He had also become adept in the art of public relations. One fine day, he disappeared from the town. He reached the capital city and revived his contacts with his forgotten relatives who stayed there. Now he was a handsome young man with good physique and sharp features. His somberness had now vanished. He was now a charming and bubbly young man. He again married into a decent and orthodox family who had fallen on bad times. He somehow obtained the agency of marketing carbon rods, used in projectors of cinema theatres, manufactured by an upcoming company, and within no time, most of the cinema theatres in the city and suburbs had become his customers.

The third boy was from a middle class peasant family who was also a neighbor of our main character. This boy was quite handsome with fair complexion. He was calm going and not used to talk unnecessarily. He had discontinued his studies after 11th standard as he had no taste for studies. He was not satisfied with the income generated from agriculture. He had other ideas to earn money, even though they could not be called humane and morale in the strict sense. He used to loan money to street venders and petty business people at a very high interest generally on day to day basis which he used to collect regularly by approaching them wherever they might be in the village at the promised time. He thus earned enough money during a short period to purchase a heavy motor goods transport vehicle. He then had begun searching for a motor transport company in the town, which was sound and honest in its dealings. He could find one such company and was successful to liaison with the company to engage his vehicle on behalf of the company for a small monthly premium. The venture had become successful and he further enlarged his business interests to other fields. You could find no substantial changes in his personality even after the amassment of a fortune, considering the fact that he had been conducting his business from the village itself.

Coming to our main character, he completed pre-university course in the town with high grades. He had not yet developed interest in general literature other than his studies. During his studies in the town, he had developed no habit of roaming around the town with classmates even during weekend holidays. He always confined himself to the college hostel and its campus. His activities were limited and routine and his thinking had not gone beyond the narrow environment that he was in. He had yet no concrete plans for the future and had yet not developed high ambitions. Even though his grandfather protested meekly against pursuing degree course in engineering, his uncle came to his rescue and got himself admitted in a reputed engineering college, as all bright students with rural background generally used to prefer engineering profession in those days.

CHAPTER 2

1964-1974

The city is one of the oldest cities in the country. It may be called a city because of the size of its population, but it more looks like a big village. The streets are not wide enough to pass two motor vehicles at the same time in opposite directions and it is better not to say anything about lanes in the interiors which are so narrow and winding that only two persons in a file can pass through the lanes. The city has a village like atmosphere with enough apparent leisure at the disposal of the citizens. The people appear to be carefree and can be seen in throngs at various places like cafes, tea stalls and small stalls engaged in selling betel leaves and tobacco, discussing about everything in the world. A high percentage of males have the habit of chewing betel leaves with tobacco and spitting on the roads. As a result the streets at most of the places have turned into red carpets. It is one of the holiest places for Hindus. The holiest river passes by the city through the plains with all its majesty and in tranquility. It is also called the city of thousand temples. You can find temples of varying sizes in every nook and corner of the city. Tourists coming to the country from outside do not miss the opportunity to visit the old city to savor its old world atmosphere. Deeply religious people from all over the country come to the city regularly to have blessings of Lord Shiva, the main deity of the city, after a dip in the holy river.

At the outskirts of the city, on the banks of the mighty river, an eminent educationist entirely on donations founded a residential university. The university is well planned and well maintained with trees blossoming with beautiful flowers of various hues in the spring season and croton plants of various shades on both sides of the roads. It is quite pleasant to the eye and refreshing to the mind as one strolls along these roads in the evenings as cool breezes of air gently touch your body while spreading fragrance of flowers. In the midst of the university, there is a beautiful temple dedicated to Lord Shiva, which is huge in proportions both horizontally and vertically with big lawns laid around the temple. The university is completely walled on all sides. It has so many disciplines of studies that one finds rarely in other universities of the country. You can call it a metropolitan university in true sense as students come from all parts of the country. But, one big blot on the face of the university is that you rarely find students from the faiths other than the Hindu religion.

An engineering college was founded in the university in the early 19th century. Our young man got himself admitted into the first year course of the five year integrated course in engineering in this college. But, the first year course was conducted out side the university in an old building with enough vacant open spaces for the students to play. In a way, it was a blessing in disguise for the fresh students as there were no senior students around to bother and irritate them, even though they had lost the lovely atmosphere of the university. There was a hostel attached to the college in the same compound.

By the time our young man entered this college, he had grown very tall but very lean. At this juncture, it is pertinent to let you know that in school days he used to wear clothes stitched by his grandmother. By the time he entered pre-university course, he was asked to wear clothes, which were borrowed from a relation of his grandmother who was fatter than him. So, during the first year of engineering, these clothes on him looked awkward and out of place. The trousers were hanging well above the heels showing part of his legs. Coupled to this, he had borrowed shoes from his uncle giving a spectacular sight to his fellow students from his province to laugh at him from behind. Here, I have to stress the fact that even though he was so peculiar and awkward to look at, he seemed to be least aware of it let alone their teasing behind him. There were about dozen students from his native province in the first year who come either from very rich families or from families having high educational back ground. He was an odd man out amongst this bunch. Most of them seemed to be interested in enjoying the freedom of being far away from their ever-guarding parents. He never felt, comfortable amongst them. But, he had no other alternative except befriending them, as he had not yet developed friendship with other students from other provinces because of constraints like language, opportunity and particularly his mental makeup. But, there was one among his native friends who maintained a cordial relationship with him who had incidentally come from a middle class family. He was thin and of very dark complexion, but had a highly mature and aristocratic look about him. We will know more about him later on.

Our young man had entered second year. Meanwhile, he had become so lazy that he used to read textbooks while lying on his bed. He had become a daydreamer, even though his dreams were incoherent and inane. However, his high level of intelligence got him through the second year without any hiccups.

Here, it is imperative to know about his unhappy experience of ragging that usually takes place in all professional colleges. Ragging in a twisted sense is said to be restored to by seniors to get themselves acquainted with or introduced to new batch of students. It might have originated from a sensible rational thinking of good intentions. But, as things generally happen in the human world, a well-formulated and well-intended custom is vulnerable to be misused by strong and devious elements without any apprehension. As it was a socially accepted evil at that period of time and also because of the laxity of authorities, elements with sadistic streak that is innate in every human being in varying degrees get aroused. Even a timid man in a group becomes strong and courageous. So, this is the most opportunistic time to satiate their pleasures which may vary from individual to individual and which may depend on the combination of several factors like heredity, upbringing, social back drop, habits, contentment etc.

One fine day, their seniors of the same province had called our bunch of friends. Everybody in the group had his own ideas about what would happen in the so-called introductory period. Nobody had any perception what actually happens during introduction as they resided far away from university and had their own world as inter mixing with the students of other provinces was minimal which would generally be maximized as time passes on and inhibitions were slowly overcome. Their stay in the college was only one month old. Their seniors assured them that the atmosphere would be cordial and there was nothing to worry. However, most of the boys were apprehensive about the coming event.

All the boys had decided to go after it was impressed upon them that it was the normal practice every year and that the attendance was compulsory. All the friends dressed up neatly and had reached the hostel in the university where their seniors reside. They nervously entered one of the rooms of the hostel to which they had been previously asked to come. Our boy was not so nervous as others, because one of the seniors belonged to his native village. At the beginning, the seniors were very polite and considerate. Introductions were completed without any hitch. Our boys had begun to feel comfortable. All of a sudden, one of the seniors had ordered our lanky boy to go below a sleeping cot, which could have been taken in a lighter vein. But unfortunately, our highly sensitive boy felt humiliated partly because of the tenor of the order and partly because of being specifically picked from so many boys. He practically had run away from the room and out of the hostel without even bothering to pick his shoes and had hurried to his room on a cycle rickshaw. While suppressing his fears of what forebodes him in the future and the anxiety of what was happening to his friends in the university, he was waiting for his friends to return. After seemingly unbearable long wait, they came disheveled and forlorn. At the beginning, they were quite indifferent and slowly began to narrate that ragging had taken a turn to worse simply because of his uncouth behavior. They were not angry with him but were very anxious about him. They had warned him that he should go to the university next morning, as otherwise the consequences would be grave when he enters the university in the second year. After much persuasion, he had gone to the same room of the university from where he was asked to go to another room upstairs where second year students were waiting for him. Their behaviour was bad and language filthy. He submitted to all their tantrums without a whimper and came down stairs to complain to a senior of his village. It had been later learnt that the second year students had been later ragged severely. He was a happy man now and soon had forgotten the trauma.

Here, I shall tell you about an extra-ordinary event that took place during his second year. The young man involved in this incident was from a highly orthodox, brahmin family from the state of Jammu & Kashmir. People from this sect of the state were generally timid and non-controversial. But this man seemed to be rebellious with communist leanings. He was short in stature but quite handsome like all the students of this sect from this province. One night, at 10 p.m., all boys of the hostel who belonged to second year were woken up out of their slumber to their bewilderment and were ordered to assemble in central courtyard with T-Squares, which were then used in engineering drawing. He alone stood in the center of circle like formation of students and began shouting and ordering the boys to perform various physical postures. However, he had been severely reprimanded by the warden the next morning. Our boy would have more contacts with him in future in the course of an extra-ordinary event that would take place because of him and some other students.

Our boy was about to open a new chapter in his life, about which he had yet no inkling, as he joined third year. In the third year he was allotted partner of a northern province. The boy was quite and calm going and was always immersed in his studies. He was of medium height with a rough face but his eyes were kind and gentle. He came from a lower middle class family. He used to bring delicious foods from his home very often as his village was not far from the university. At this point of time, our boy came across a personality who was a friend of his roommate. He came from a highly orthodox medium class family. He was gentle in behavior and soft in speech. He was of medium height and of very fair complexion. He had not been studious of late because of a failed love affair and he had not been unable to pass the hurdle of third year examination since two years. He introduced our boy to literature and persuaded him to read religisous books specially those written by Swami Vivekananda and Ramakrishna Paramahamsa. He was deeply moved by the sayings of Ramakrishna. The saying of Ramakrishna that without under going suffering and hardships one could not realize God just like that butter could not be materialized without thorough churning of curd.

Later on, our boy took deep interest in literature of western writers, which were readily available to him from the small private library of his uncle who resided on the other side of the river in the residential quarters of a factory located at about five kilometer from the bank of the river. His uncle was tall and well built with a handsome and charming face. His behavior towards our young man was gentle and kind and he was so confident of our young man that he was not in the habit of enquiring about either his studies or his activities in the university. His aunt talked to him very rarely until unless it was absolutely necessary. She was very adept in preparing delicious dishes. To go to this place from the university, it was cheaper and time saving to cross the river by a boat and then hire a rickshaw. He was in the habit of going to this place very often.

Our young man was getting engrossed in spiritual quest. He was quite puzzled and disturbed by the explanations and theories of the past and the present proposed by spiritual and religious luminaries, as they were unable to solve the puzzles generated by his rational thinking in his own perspective. But his pursuit to find his own answers was not continual but was occasional as and when he was inclined to think in that direction when he was alone. Because of this deviation, he barely got through the third year. In spite of all this, pleasant changes were taking place in his personality. Because of the self-confidence generated due to exposure to various forms of literature and new found friends who cared for him, his timidity and aloofness were giving way to courage and extrovert ness.

During the fourth year, he had been shifted to another hostel. This time his room partner was a tall and stout young man coming from a near by district, who hailed from a class whose ancestors were warriors. He had a long drooping nose and a wide mouth. His face was oblong with depressed spots on the cheeks and a thin moustache along the upper lip. He gave a first impression of tough and rough guy. He was highly emotional and gets furious on slightest provocation. But, his behavior towards our young man was decent and amicable.

During this period, on one of his occasional journeys to his uncle's house, his eyes had fallen upon a book about Mr. Gandhi, which had been edited by a lady called Mrs. Burke. He was so stirred by the book and by the personality of Mr. Gandhi as depicted on the book with so much intensity and sincerity, that a complete transformation had taken place in his personality within no time. He had parted ways with his trousers and shirts and had begum to wear pyjamas made of thin cotton cloth and long kurtas made from hand woven clothes. He also disowned thick bed filled with cotton wool as well as sandals. His transformation was so smooth and quick and he was so convinced of his transformation that he had begum to wonder whether becoming a great human being was such a simple affair. Now, this kind of thinking shows that a certain measure of pride was developing in him, which might lead to arrogance stunting the growth. Here, we had to stress the fact that certain basic qualities already imbibed in him combined with strong convictions in his own life style giving least importance to the mocking attitude of others must have contributed to the genuine transformation in such a quick time. And of course, there was continuous streak of bewilderment growing in him about the in-equalities in the live species of Nature.

On one of these days, his roommate had breezily entered the room and started cursing a certain professor. On enquiry, it was revealed to him that he and two other students had been debarred from appearing the final examination of fourth year at the recommendation of the mathematics professor. He further informed that the professor had put secret symbolic signs on the answer books of home assignments earlier submitted by some students. Without being aware of this, our friends resubmitted answer books of three of these students interchanging the names on the covers by pasting a slip of paper. It appeared that the professor had been aware of this mischief of these students since some time. Generally, most of the students and professors gave no significant importance to the home assignments knowing pretty well that very few students completed the assignment on their own and that the rest just copied. However, it was made to understand that these students had unintentionally slighted the professor recently and the professor was waiting for the kill. It was a common perception that uneducated village folk in general were innocuous and the urbane educated were imprudent and impulsive while addressing personal grievances. It so happened that the professor had soon got the opportunity to implicate them on serious charges of copying and got them debarred from appearing in the examinations.

The room partner was highly agitated and furious and was threatening to assault the professor. It would be unfair on my part if I miss telling that the partner was more intelligent and studious than our young man. He reached this far after obtaining first class grades in the first three years. If he were to repeat the year again, his pride would be hurt and would not be able to show his face to his parents to his village folk and to his friends. The second debarred man was also studying in fourth year but in some other branch. He was the Kashmiri boy who had conducted mass ragging while our young man had been in second year. As we already knew that this youth was also short tempered and rebellious. He was just selected as a short service commissioned officer in the Army. His selection would be cancelled if the suspension were not revoked. The third boy was of no consequence as be had been in that year since a long time.

Leaving alone the merits and demerits of the case, our young man had become apprehensive about his partner's intentions. He was pacifying his partner while pondering over to find an amicable solution. He naturally decided to go on an indefinite hunger strike till the suspension orders are rescinded. It was about 9 pm when the decision was taken by which time our man had his dinner. Simultaneously, notice of indefinite hunger strike was dispatched to the vice-chancellor and to the director of the institute informing them about the commencement of the hunger strike that would be continued till the orders of ban on the three students were rescinded since the act of omission committed by them was not grave enough to warrant such a punishment. He sat on a table in the recreation room whole night but for occasional loosening of the limbs by spreading himself on the table without any out side disturbance.

At around 7 am in the next morning, the warden of the hostel had approached him and ordered him to leave the reading room immediately as this was not the place to indulge in such activities. He calmly had gone outside the hostel and had stood below a small tree on the other side of the road just opposite the hostel gate. It may be mentioned here that not a single student including the three boys had met him after the start of the hunger strike, because he unequivocally told them the previous night that he desired to deal with the matter alone and he also chided them for their contemptuous attitude towards the particular professor. It was now 8.30 a.m. and he had been standing there since one and half hour. Students one by one, started going to the college and soon students in batches had started pouring on to the roads leading to the college. The students were looking fresh with scrubbed faces and trim with immaculate dresses and polished shoes. In contrast, the eyes of our boy were glowing red with a sleepless night behind; the hair disheveled for want of oiling and combing; the clothes dirty because of the dust on the table and crumpled because of the cotton fabric; a not so clean towel around his neck; a tiring look with un shaven face with stubs of hair on his cheeks; sunken eyes and cheeks, and bare feet. He looked like a perfect example of a wayward wanderer without food or sleep or shelter for many days. They were neither curious nor there were any enquiring glances from any of the students passing by him. In fact nobody seemed to be interested. But, he stood there unruffled.

At 9 p.m., the warden of the hostel came from the college to inform him that the director of the institute had called him and was waiting in his chambers. Our man, whose figure must be embarrassing to any authority to talk to, had slowly walked to the chambers of the director. The director politely invited him into his chambers where some other professors of the institute had already been seated. Our controversial professor stood in the verandah in front of the chambers. The director was an old man of about 58 years of age hailing from an eastern province. His eyes seemed to be penetrating into you. The director softly enquired from the boy about the purpose of his hunger strike. There was no trace of anger or irritation in his voice. The appearance of the boy seemed to perturb him the least. He might have already gathered sufficient information about the boy. That could have made it easier for the boy in having a good rapport with the director in a short time. Our boy, while agreeing with the director and other professors that an amoral conduct was committed by the debarred students, had emphasized that the act was cunningly unveiled by the professor because of some previous grouse against the students and that this slip of the students was not grave enough to warrant suspension and that most of the students including him had often resorted to copying the home assignments from the record books of other students and that the guilty students had expressed their repentance. The director was thoughtful for a seemingly long minute and smiled at our boy. The director had passed orders to lift the suspension orders and allow the students to appear in the final examinations. The director was so impressed by our boy that he invited the boy to his house at his own convenience. Overwhelmed by the fast developments in the favor of students and the graciousness of the director, our boy not only had given in writing withdrawing his hunger strike but also impulsively announced that he would not appear in the ensuing final examinations. That was just rubbing salt in the wound. The three students already humiliated by the turn of events were now completely dazed. It took one month for them to decide not to appear in the examinations and to repeat the entire academic year. Our young man would be knowing in future that how his impulsive decision had put brakes to his smooth academic progress in spite of his declining interest in the engineering studies. The Kashmiri student had become deeply religious and was now a regular visitor to the temples wearing a big insignia on his fore head. The room partner of our boy had become sedate and dignified.

Now, what had been happening to our young man? He was in a complete dilemma of what to do next. His goals had no physical barriers and not limited to any particular sphere of activity and they are not only hard to realize but also might be impossible to attain of which he was certainly aware of. On a fine morning, he had decided to leave the university once for all. At about 8.00 am, he walked out of the university with only ten rupees in cash in his pocket and without any bag and baggage and without informing any body. He walked out of the city along a highway that came in his path with no specific direction in mind. He continued walking on the highway through highly fertile deltaic lands and villages till 2.00 p.m. He then took a light breakfast at a roadside eatery in a small village and took off again. As he was walking through the villages, he felt envious looking at the people secure in their abodes with a feeling of apparent contentment showing an their faces. At this point, it could be honestly implied our boy was still unable to break out of the chains of a happy social life. Still, he continued his journey. Soon it was dusk and the sun was slowly going behind the horizon.

At a point of the highway, he broke off from the highway and started to walk in a perpendicular direction. After some time, he realized that a strange smell was emitting from the ground and soon he realized that it was a graveyard. He suddenly took a u-turn and started walking fast along the same highway he had previously treaded upon and reached the university by about 4.00 a.m. the next morning. None of his friends were aware of his aimless sojourn. He had now dispensed with his present mode of dress and reverted back to normal ways.

He had not appeared in the examinations of the fourth year and took re-admission into the fourth year course of the engineering. By now, he had become a brave and courageous man and all his previous inhibitions and shyness were now completely over come. The fresh batch of fourth year students was allotted one of the four wings of another hostel in the first floor. There were only two rooms in the wing, which were not yet filled up. In each of these two rooms, only one student was presently staying. One was a big long room by the side of the staircase with no proper ventilation. On enquiry, he had been informed that no body dared to approach the resident of the second room with an intention of sharing it. However, one a fine evening, our man had approached the room and gave a light knock on the door. A hefty man of medium height with a rotund face and fierce eyes with a very thick moustache, which was curled upward at its ends, opened the door and calmly enquired about the purpose of the disturbance. Our young man simply told him of his intention to share the room with him. Without any hesitation and without any annoyance showing on his face, he politely invited our man to become his room partner.

Here, we should know something about the general environment and polity of the university.

In the olden days, large chunks of enrolment in the professional and postgraduate courses had been from urban middle class society with high educational family background and aristocratic bent of mind. These students had a good command of English and were highly polished in their behavior. These people were habituated to treat the students with rural background shabbily. With the passage of time, students from the villages of northern province, in which the university was located, started to get admitted into these course on merit in large numbers.

Students in the non-professional under graduate course were generally locals and did not stay in the hostels of the university.

The urbane people looked down the rural students with disdain who were coarse in their speech and manners. The rural students hailing from warrior class were more offended than anybody else by this kind of demeanor. Certain professors of this class were really agitated by this type of discrimination towards their brethren. They were waiting for an opportune time to teach a lesson to these students especially to those who put on lot of airs. This batch of Raj puts who were co-students of our hefty man in his class, were well built and muscular and hailed from rich agricultural families. They were courageous and daring and did not have the timidity or shyness or tolerance or assimilating quality of their senior brethren. They had formed a group with our hefty man as their head. This room partner of our young man came from a highly educated family whose father was working as a professor in the only university in Kathmandu. This man was daring and dashing. His small eyes were always piercing and suspicious. Now and then, one could observe traces of ferociousness in these eyes. This group initially started to treat the urbane students with derisiveness. Soon, with the patronage of some professors and politicians, they had gathered enough courage to manhandle anybody who they think had misbehaved with their brethren. Soon, their activities reached such a crescendo that the group became the most dreaded group in the university.

There were three active student groups in the university. The most popular among the students was the socialist group led by a lean and short man hailing from an eastern province. The second group, which was most influential among the authorities, belonged to a Hindu extremist group, which was highly active in the university having its own official office room. The third group though small in numbers, had extremist communistic bearings. This group used to hold secret meetings to enlighten themselves and to assess the activities of the movement in the entire country. The leader of this group was a short, dark and thin man, with a brass tone. His mother worked as a cook in the house of a professor. He was an highly emotional man and was doing his post graduation course in social sciences. Besides our dreaded group, the students belonging to Hindu extremist group were also feared for they were highly united and had also the patronage of politicians and authorities. If anybody outside of this group misbehaves with any one of their brethren, this group immediately springs into action and a batch of students of R.S.S. residing nearer to the scene reaches the scene of action in no time and pursues the guilty till they were caught and beaten up black and blue. So, no student dared to offend them.

In one of the annual elections to the students union of the university, a president contestant supported by the group belonging to our hefty man was defeated. The group had come to the conclusion that the entire student community haling from a southern province of a particular college had not voted for their candidate in spite of their promise, which was usually given to all contestants, and blamed this student community for the defeat even though as per actual statistics and the margin of the result, the votes of this group would have made little difference. One day, in the middle of the night, this group consisting of about 50 students had entered the hostel in which this particular student community resided. They bolted the doors of all the rooms from outside and started beating them one by one black and blue by forcing them to open the doors from inside. Before the students were aware of what was happening they completed the job and had left the hostel as fast as they had come. But, no body including student leaders and teaching staff dared to protest against the atrocity. The authorities kept mum and the reasons for such attitude were well known to all. But, there was one exception. The socialist leader of socialist leanings had protested with no result. Though he was lean and short, his voice rang like a bell and he was a fluent speaker. He was one person who was not afraid of this group even though he had been beaten several times severely but escaped each time from jaws of death simply because of the wishes of the group to let him live. Still, he continued to take active interest in the affairs of students.

Rarely, leaders without affiliation to any group or faction had sprung up. But one such rare student was slowly and steadily taking roots. He had graduated from the engineering college of the same university and was doing his post-graduation course. He was a judo wrestler. He was a very hefty and muscular personality. He used to speak softly and used to behave politely with one and all. He hailed from one of the northern most provinces. After sustained efforts of campaigning, he had been elected student union leader. But, the joy of the majority of the students was short lived as he had been stabbed to death in the darkness of one late evening when he was strolling on the road alone. No body could be apprehended, as there was no evidence.

Our young man was living with the leader of the most dreaded group of the university. The behavior of the leader towards our young man was always polite and he was the first person to wish our young man every morning. But, our man behaved as though none existed in the room and was always immersed in his own intensive meditative like thinking without attending classes and not even bothering to take food. Again on one day, our man had gone on one of his fruitless and purposeless journeys and has come back after two days. Within a week of his coming, first semester examinations were due to be held. Our man got into the job immediately and got through the examinations to the surprise of one and all. His partner was both perplexed and amused by his way of life. Now, the leader began introspection and a long inner conflict had ensued.

During this period of time, a young brash boy studying in the first year of engineering, who belonged to the sect of the leader used to frequently come to his room. This boy of the younger generation was more sophisticated and cultured than his predecessors but the violent temper and egoistic tendencies of his predecessors remained intact in his genes also. Our man was never used to speak to him. He was being groomed as the future leader of the group.

One day, our aristocratic looking black complexioned man from the native province of our man introduced a young chap, who had newly joined the first year of engineering and hailed from the same province. The friend of our young man informed him that the boy was about to run away from the university to his native place being afraid of ragging. His friend had requested him to take the boy under his guard till the intensity of ragging had waned. Our young man had asked the boy to spend the nights in his room and informed him that he need no longer worry about ragging. The boy had become self-assured and self-confidence seemed to have returned. Our man could at the same time discern that some traces of misplaced arrogance had crept into him. One day, the boy had a small altercation with the brash boy who regularly visits the leader and the brash boy slapped him during the altercation. It seemed that psychology of our boy has changed after the incident and he was no longer worried about ragging and kept himself to his room.

As already informed, the leader had begum introspection and an inner conflict had ensued in him. He began to think that here was a man who never bothered about himself and did not seem to be least afraid of him and that he was highly intelligent and that if he so desires, he could easily top the class. He always thought of others. But what he was doing? He always flaunted himself of being the most important person in the university. But what purpose did it serve? No body dared to come near to him or talk to him except those belonging to his group. His main activity was to look for opportunity to antagonize, and manhandle students. He was doing justice neither to his studies nor to himself. He was being looked upon as an untouchable by most of the students. Living with this kind of man for a man like him was becoming increasingly unbearable and mentally torturous. One day he talked to his group about disbanding the group for which the group had not agreed to. He informed his room partner about their intentions and that they might physically assault him. Our young man had assured him that he need not fear anybody as long as he was with him. This assurance so dazzled him and put utter bewilderment in his egoistic mind that he at once decided to quit from hoodlumism and the dreaded group and to face any consequences that might arise from his decision.

Our young man had not appeared in the second semester examination of fourth year and again rejoined fourth year. During this second stint of the fourth year, his friend from the central province used to come to his room not very often simply because of his abhorrence towards his partner. Whenever he came, his stay was very brief. He used to enquire about our young man and used to give instructions to the chief chef of the mess to take responsibility of providing food to him regularly as he was so absentminded that he was least aware of his surroundings and used to forget even taking food often.

In the third stint of fourth year, he had been provided with a separate room in another hostel. Here he had come in close contact with two friends of his caring friend. One student was in fourth year of electrical engineering. He was a well-built boy of brown complexion coming from a business family of central province. He had a look of careless ness about everything and used to take things lightly. He was a brilliant boy and have vibrant and joyous nature. The second boy was also in the fifth year of the same branch. He was of very peculiar character. He was of medium height and fair complexion and seemed to be too young to his age. He was talkative and used to indulge in peculiar activities that created mirth from the people. These three people were now and then engaged in petty quarrels and used to complain to our boy. They were also habituated to tell lies while narrating their complaints to our boy. Our young man used to wonder why they unnecessary quarreled among themselves on petty issues and told all sorts of lies to camouflage their mistakes. He used to wonder that why any body at all told lies. After a long period, he would realize that how intoxicating the lies were. These people had become close friends. Now our man was gradually coming out of his hibernation and started enjoying life as it comes by. But his frame of mind was not suited to that type of life. He again took to reading. He had read several books of some eminent authors of French, Russian and English literature. The complexities of human nature and the conflicts and the sufferings consequent there upon had bewildered and disturbed him so much that he had again gone in to deep hibernation. The saying of Ramakrishna was still nagging his mind occasionally.

One day he decided to go on his final voyage. He had worn loose trousers made of thin cotton cloth and a shirt and placed a thin towel on his shoulders and had kept only two rupees in cash with him. The period of time was mid summer. The weather was very hot and dry and by afternoon strong winds, which were very hot, were blowing across continually. He had set on his journey at about 6 a.m. and reached a railway station 10 km., from the city at about 8 a.m. Here he came across an incident, which would be imbibed, in his mind forever. In front of the railways station at a secluded corner by the side of a passenger shelter, there on the ground lay a thick circular container made of vegetable leaves containing some food probably thrown away by some passengers without completely consuming the food. On one side of the leaf sat a dog on its hinds, which appeared to be very hungry. The bones were showing off the skin and stomach was highly depressed. In its eyes one can observe fear of the thought that the food might be snatched away any moment and arising from the fear, a look of anger and ferociousness had crept into his eyes to put freight into his enemy. On the other side of the leaf, a thin, bony old man looking more like a skeleton stood. He also seemed to be very hungry and very eager to snatch the food. For some seemingly long seconds no body seemed to be dare enough to take initiative. Suddenly the dog took a lunge at the man with a growl. The old man trying to evade and some how intending to snatch the leaf, took a small stick lying near by and tried to hit the dog and the dog more ferocious now took a leap at the man with an intention of biting and clawing. In the ensuing struggle the food had been scattered around on the ground. They were fighting a purposeless duel with no one a winner.

It may be neither superficial nor out of place to magnify the event and un-equivocally state that the event reflected the status of lower middle class and weakest in the country even after the advent of independence and democracy in the country, which was 25 years old. Not surprisingly, communist party, which had genesis of dictatorship mode of administration, had taken strong roots in the most literate state of the country. Naxalism, an extremist communist organization, which believed in transformation of the society through and barrel of the gun, had sprung up in the most talented and articulate province of the country. It might be construed that the minimum basic needs and desires of the weaker sections of the society were far from fulfillment. The political administration and beaurocracy of the nation were dominated by the rich and aristocrats who had neither the awareness of the turmoil of the week nor the foresightedness to uplift them with radical measures which were essential under the circumstances. No attempts were made to contain corruption, which was beginning to rear its ugly head and smugglers who had taken deep roots through out the country. At this point of time, a radical leader with high innovativeness with only formal education took reins of the country.

Our man had continued his journey from the railway station towards eastern direction along a national highway. At about 2 pm., he had become thirsty and knocked on one of the doors of a thatched house of a small village by the highway. An old woman with eyes full of kindness and a gentle smile opened the doors and brought water in a big brass glass along with sweets and gently offered him. He took them with gratification and seemed to be sufficiently energized to continue his journey. He had walked along the highway till about 5 p.m. There was a big village some distance away from the highway. He took a detour and entered the village and took some eatables that could be purchased with two rupees in his pocket at a small eatery and passed through the village to its outskirts. There he sat below a big tree and ate the food he bought. After some time a villager passing by had approached him and requested him to come to the village to have some food and rest, as he appeared to the villager very hungry and tired. But our young man had kept quite and the villager had gone away.

He sat there for about two hours until there was complete darkness. He had then gone further into fields and after assuring himself that nobody would pass by, had removed all his clothes and searched around for thorny bushes. He soon found them near by and had broken away some dry branches on the ground and laid on them. He closed his eyes and tried to be as calm as he could be and not allowed any extraneous thoughts to enter his mind. There was complete silence all round. After an hour or so, there was a sudden rustling sound near by. A kind of involuntary fear had crept through his spine nay for a moment. That had been enough for him to come to instantaneous conclusion that he was unfit for the journey. He later observed that a stream was passing by and the sound had been because of an animal getting into the stream to drink water.

He immediately decided to go to his abode. He had put on his clothes. He was not aware of the time as he had not brought his watch with him. He had no inkling of the path or direction he had to take, as it was completely dark and it was one of those moonless nights. Nothing was visible. He had begun to walk blindly through fields hoping that he was in the right direction to reach the highway. But alas the he had chosen a wrong direction. There was no sight of highway in spite of several hours of treading through bushes, marshy lands, wet agricultural fields with a nagging fear of treading on poisonous snakes. At last he could see to his delight lights speeding past far away. It was almost dawn before he reached the highway. The sunrays were just emerging out of the horizon. He could distinguish a factory near the highway and a pond about hundred feet away. People were not yet observed either near the highway or in the vicinity out side the walled factory. By now our man was so much exhausted that he almost fainted on the kerb of the road. He was unable to stand on his legs and he was feeling very thirsty. He crawled towards the pond slowly and observed that water was at a low level and was dirty. Probably the waters had become dirty because of the effluents from the factory and the nature of effluents was not known. There was no alternative to him except to drink the water to escape fainting on the road. He crawled to the edge of the water and slowly begun to drink enough water to quench his thirst. He now regained some energy and was able to stand on his legs. There was a big banyan tree near the pond. The sun was slowly emerging out of the horizon and he was able to distinguish objects far away. Luckily for him the factory was an ice-manufacturing factory. He could observe agricultural fields at two hundred meters away. He slowly walked to the fields where he observed clean water flowing through open concrete lined feeder channel. He drank the water by lifting them with cupped hands till his stomach was full. He regained enough energy and the body was now relaxed. He removed his upper garments and wrapped the thin towel around his buttocks. Now, the sky is completely lit and people from the village started coming out for their daily chores.

He then washed his clothes and under garments and spread them on the sugarcane plants in the fields. He kept on waiting for them to be dried. The clothes dried sooner than anticipated as the wind was blowing. He washed his towel, which also dried in no time. He wore the clothes and reached the highway.

One vendor was selling eatables and tea beneath the banyan tree. By his sheer luck, the place happened to be a stop for passenger buses. There were already several people standing there to board the buses. He approached a gentleman who was well dressed and appeared to be educated. He acquainted him about his background and about his present plight. The gentleman was wise and seemed to be convinced. But to be completely satisfied, the gentleman asked our young man some questions pertaining to physical sciences. When he was satisfied with the replies, he gave the young man ten rupees in cash, which was enough to enable him to reach the university, and also ordered the vendor to give the young man some eatables. After consuming the eatables, he thanked the gentle man profusely and boarded a bus that was headed for the city. He reached his room in the university at about 10.00 a.m. His friends had been anxiously searching for him and were delighted to see him back at last. But by the evening, he had been afflicted with virus fever. He had been immediately admitted in the emergency ward of the university hospital and by the next morning his condition had vastly improved even though the weakness in the body had not completely left him. Supplementary examinations of the second semester were fast approaching and were scheduled to be commenced after seven days. Permission had been granted to write examinations in the hospital under the supervision of an invigilator specially appointed for the purpose. The examinations were completed to his full satisfaction.

Here, it is to be informed that from the fifth year of his residence in the university, he stopped going to his native place in summer vacations. His uncle also got new postings in a factory in the capital of his province in the same year. He stopped taking money from his uncle for certain reasons which are not relevant to be revealed here and the entire expenditure towards his education from now onwards fell on the shoulders of his grandfather. With rains failing frequently and the income from agriculture bring meager, his grandfather had been placed in a piquant situation combined with a feeling that his grandson had gone awry and that he was unsure of his grandson's sincerity towards his studies. He was hesitant to take loans to meet the expenditure of our young man. The young man did not receive money through money orders regularly. Even the money he received as and when it was sent was not even sufficient to cater to the needs of food leave alone college and hostel fees. All his close friends of the institute had left the university after completing the studies. Under this unpleasant ambience, he entered the final year of his degree course. As the occasional money he received from his grand parents was meager to meet the food bill either in the hostel mess or in the canteen, he joined the mess in a village nearer to the university with the help of a friend, where poor students had their meals. The food was cheap but nourishing and tasty.

His classmates in the final year were too young to have close relationship. He used to spend most of his leisure time reading literature and occasionally indulging in playing indoor games. It was not that much difficult to spend time with the students moving around in the hostel and in the university campus. But once the summer vacation started almost all the students used to leave the place to be at home and the hostels were almost empty. During these periods, he used to feel so lonely that at times a feeling of restlessness and craziness used to creep in to him, though occasionally, when the time seemed to be not moving.

Man is a social animal. He cannot live alone in a lonely place for a long time and much more so when there is no stimulating activity, which even is true even for an insane human being. The mind is such that it needs occasional pleasantness and refreshness to its own liking to function normally even in great turmoil. A man is normally capable of assimilating all kinds of physical and mental sufferings given that he gets diverted to occasional pleasures in the course of his life. But, prolonged loneliness in a secluded place is just unbearable even if it is objective. All the more, sudden loneliness is such a punishment to both mind and body that might result in abnormalities in man's physic. He had felt one such abnormal psychological aberration during this period. At times during the night, while he was in his room, even a slight sound used to become magnified several times to his ears. He was so afraid that he immediately used to come out of his room and walked in the corridor. For some seconds, even his footsteps used to sound like big thuds. After a few minutes, the abnormal sound sense used to come back to normality. Then only, he could master enough courage to enter the room again.

He could not appear in the final examination of the fifth year, as he had not paid the tuition fees as well as examination fee. He had to repeat the final year again. During this period of second stint of final year, it was quite appropriate to recreate an incident that happened in his hostel, which reflected the psychology of some of the students, which often borders on cynicism, sadism and arrogance and unwanted heroism without any heroics towards lesser-privileged people.

One day, it was observed that a wristwatch of a particular student had been missing from his room. The blame had been squarely placed on a mess boy in whom the student was a member. The alleged culprit was an unbelievably handsome boy in his teens and of very fair complexion. He was well built without being muscular and about two inches taller than the average height. His skin was fine textured and glowing. His eyes were big exuberating gentleness and a kind of innocence that was generally observed in some un-educated village folk. His nose was straight and beautifully rounded at the nostrils and the lips were rose pink in color with delicate and well shaped sprouts of flesh lowering into the mouth with the upper lips slightly curved at the ends. His looks were so arresting and pleasing to the eyes that it was difficult to suppress one's desire to kiss him.

He had been called to the room of the student whose watch was missing. The news was spread fast around and about a dozen students gathered in the room in no time. The boy slowly walked in to the room without the least idea of what the students were up to. When the boy was asked sternly by one of the students to sit on his knees, the thought that something was amiss and that he was in deep trouble suddenly flashed through his mind. He sat on the knees, his face now pale and eyes lowered with thin layers of liquid already covering them. The gleam in the eyes of some of the students had sent shivers through his spine. His plight could be compared to the agony of a beautiful deer in front of a tiger, fully aware that he was going to serve as food for the tiger in few seconds. The students shouted at him and demanded to bring the watch he had stolen. With words difficult to come by, the boy expressed his innocence. Simultaneously, a student who had a ring on the middle finger of the left hand struck violently with his knuckles on the head of the boy. Instantly tears began to roll out of his eyes on to the cheeks. The boy kept mum. Another student slapped with all his strength on the left cheek of the boy and demanded to bring the ring. The boy had no answer to give expect to grumble that he was innocent. Another student took sandals and started hitting the boy with no particular target in the mind. Now the blood started slowly oozing out of his nostrils in drops. You could observe a kind of sadistic gleam in the eyes of the students and abhorring delight on their faces. They seemed to be least bothered at the loss of the watch at the moment but only in satiating their sadistic pleasures. After sometime, they asked the boy to leave the room and the watch had not been traced.

During summer vacations after the ninth academic year of his staying in the university, preceding his second stint in final year, summons had come from his grandfather to come over to them immediately to see a girl, who according to their message looked like his sister, and to marry her if he so desires. He had no alternative except to embark on a long journey after a long time. The formal get to know each other meeting was arranged in a town nearer to his paternal grand parents village in the house of the girl's elder sister. The boy along with his grand mother and his uncle reached the house. The girl's father was thin, tall and dark. He seemed to be not only gentle and simple but also submissive by nature even though he hailed from a rich family whose father was once the chairman of the municipality of the town and had relatives holding top positions in their field of activities. The young man was neither aware of the background of her family nor about the wealth of the family at that time and he was least interested to know about their background. The girl's father led the boy and his relatives into a well-decorated small room where some people sat on the mat lay on the ground. Two young boys were briskly moving hither and thither looking after the needs of the guests. The boys, it was told, were brothers of the girl, who though were very dark complexioned were looking quite handsome with well built limbs and pleasant faces with sharp features. A very fat girl with dark complexion and with fat rotund face with wide nostrils sat on the floor with face lowered a bit towards the ground. Our young man was more fascinated by the two young boys and had just a glimpse of the girl and immediately conveyed his willingness to marry her even though his uncle tried to stop him from the declaration with the intent of thinking it over at their home before making any hasty decision. But it was too late. The marriage was arranged in the most sacred temple of the country and by the end of the month they were married. Here it was important to inform that he was given Rs. 20,000 in cash towards marriage expenses. Half the amount was spent on the marriage. He deposited about Rs. 5000 in a bank of the town nearer to his village and came back to the university with Rs. 5000 in cash. His personality was now completely changed with costly clothes around his body and gold ring around his index finger that were bought by his in laws. He cleared all the dues pending against him in the college and the hostel as well as the canteen. He was now a very happy man. His past time indulgence in spiritual odyssey vanished, though temporarily. He joined a mess in the hostel and it seemed as though that happy days had come to him at last. He passed the final year examinations and at last completed his engineering course in the university. Before ending up his sojourn in the university, it is relevant and highly essential to know the gradual changes that had taken place in his physic during this period that would have a bearing on the events that would take place in his life during the course of time.

An unassuming, innocent and shy man when he joined the engineering course had gradually developed into a self assured and motivated courageous young man who still was usually quite and clam and pleasing in his demeanors. He still had not yet developed any deep attachment to any physical entity, which persisted for a long time. Then gradually, his self confidence and his belief in his intelligence in analyzing things and self righteousness coupled with a nagging unconscious sense of insecurity in life and financial constraints had become catalysts to make him some what haughty and intolerant in nature leading to fits of anger and misplaced emotions at times.

CHAPTER 3

1974-1979

The dynamic leader with formal education who took the reins of the country gradually consolidated her position in the party and became the undisputed leader of the party and the country. The leader was starting to be recognized as the messiah of the down trodden and scheduled castes. Accolades were showered upon her by both upper and lower casts of the society for her daring reforms in agricultural, land ceiling, banking sector and for the actions initiated to achieve the desired goals, which were very affective and fruitful especially in the upliftment of scheduled castes.

But, alas, people were in for a rude jolt when suddenly, without any inkling of what was to be expected the next day, internal emergency was imposed throughout the country, for an entirely obscure reason which would have been tackled with coolness & deftness coupled with some little prudence that were required from a seasoned politician, who had already been ruling the country for the past 10 years. The later day events would expose the tyrannical attitude of the ruler as well as the ambition in all its morbidity to stick to power. The tenure of the central assembly has been extended to two years under representatives of peoples act. At last good sense prevailed and general elections had been ordered to be conducted. The opposition parties despite their ideological differences merged themselves into one single party and won general elections with comfortable majority. But soon, the ideological differences prevailed over the political bond and necessity to survive took a back seat in spite of the harsh experiences the leaders and people had gone through during that black period. The

Govt. tumbled like a pack of cards and general elections were again held and in these elections the leader of whom we were talking about came back to power with thumping majority showing the resilience and flexibility of the mind of the people of the country who did not want a hotch potch Government and prepared to give a chance to the debased leader on the promise of giving a good Govt. and not imposing internal emergency again.

Unfortunately, this time the leader wrested the power with vastly changed attitudes towards life and society. It can be affirmed that during this subsequent period, seeds of corruption as an un-avoidable social evil were sown which would grow into mammoth proportions in the decades to come by. During the period of emergency, our young man joined an engineering department of the state Govt. as a junior engineer. Whenever he thought of the emergency, the first thing that came to his to mind was about the fate of the lean and dark extremist minded student of the university, as those days became very difficult for such persons to survive.

The unit to which he had been posted was responsible for the estimation of structures that would come under submergence under the reservoir of a hydroelectric scheme, which was under construction in addition to the designs of the scheme.

He had been reposted to a sub-division located in a village about 70 km from the project site and about 30 km from the district head quarters. The village was the headquarters of a Taluk. As such, all the basic facilities were available in the village except a suitable house to get on rent specially for the people hailing from the rich coastal districts. The houses in these parts of the state were of peculiar construction. The rooms of the houses were generally compartmental in orientation unlike those in coastal belt. The most disturbing aspect of the houses was the nature of roof construction. Stone slabs were first placed with tight joints on the timber beams narrowly spaced. On these slabs, a thick layer of a mixture of earth and dried leaves was spread neatly and evenly over which a thick layer of cement mortar was laid. Even though, the roof was generally waterproof, problems crept up often because of the middle layer. Over the years, the middle layer became the breeding ground for several types of insects including poisonous scorpions.

The sub-division to which he was reposted was mainly responsible for estimating the structures that would be started submerging under the reservoir of the scheme once the level of the dam reaches to a certain pre-determined level. The sub division was run by a head of the rank of Asst Engineer and five section officers including our young man, a clerk and a draughtsman working under him. The sub-division had an old jeep to take the staff to the affected villages.

On the first day he the joined duty, he was handed over 70 Rupees in cash with the information that it was his share for the present. Our young man had the least idea of what his colleagues were talking about but had pocketed the money without asking any questions, which he thought was not prudent enough at that time. The very next day he was requested to give a party to all the technical staff of the sub-division as a token of good gesture. He had to cough about 100 rupees for the party, which incidentally included the 70 rupees he was given the previous day the reasons for which act were still unknown to him.

After two days, the staff including our young man had gone to one of the affected villages to take necessary measurements and accounting of all the required features of some of the houses costing more than Rs. 25,000/-in order to prepare detailed estimates of the costs of the houses. Even though unskilled workers from outside could be hired to help in taking measurements, the staff had taken the necessary measurements by distributing the work among themselves and with the help of office attender and driver of the jeep. The job was completed by noon. The head of the village arranged a lavish lunch in this house. They chitchatted for a while after the lunch and left the village to their headquarters in a congenial atmosphere. After one week of the journey, our young man was given printed proformae filled with some names of persons supposedly engaged in the previously mentioned job, called nominal master roll, to attest in evidence of utilizing them by him in this work. Our young man politely refused to comply with the request.

But to his dismay, they stopped taking him to the affected villages and no field work was entrusted to him from then onwards. He used to pass the time by seeing movies once in a week, which was the duration a movie was exhibited, in the only cinema theatre in the village and occasional office work that came by his way but most of the time spent in idling. The only delightful moments for him in that period were when he went to a mess in the village for breakfast. A couple in advanced age ran the mess with no extra help from outside. There was one dish on the menu of the hotel, which was so tasty and delightful to savor that people used to wait for an hour to get their turn. Our young man used to look forward for these moments every morning. The dish was called 'Ravvattu' which was a mixture of maida and curd spread uniformly on a big oven in a thin layer and roasted with oil slowly to the specifications. But the delightful taste was actually felt when roasted attu was taken along with chutney which combined with it so beautifully to enhance the taste to sublime levels.

In the village, there were two other sub-divisions engaged in similar work as that of the sub-division of our young man. One day, a section officer from one of these divisions approached him and desired to suggest him ways and means to boost the estimating of the houses. Our young man was at first hesitant but after continuous prodding and besieging had agreed to give suggestions for boosting the estimating of the houses. The suggestions of our young man were very simple in nature. He advised him that without changing the total plinth area of the house and specifications of supporting walls and roof, the foundations could be shown more deeper than actual, and some of the country wood doors and windows could be shown as of teak wood, the no of beams supporting the roof could be increased depending upon the size of the house, without any risk of getting caught up to the level of head of the sub-division who would be certainly involved in the mischief and to some extent by the head of the division who was required to check measure only 25% of the measurements. Even if some deviations were observed during the inspection of the divisional officer, no action would be taken except giving hollow warnings and he would correct the deviations without any hassle, as he was also a part and parcel of the same system. The officer gave our young man Rs. 700/-for these suggestions. At that minute, a thought flashed through his mind if graduated engineers like him, who were neither honest nor intelligent at the beginning of their service itself, were to be elevated to higher echelons in the organization in due course of time, which would happen in a routine manner in Govt. service, the fate of the department in near by future could be gruesome.

Here It was to be mentioned that one day while standing near by a cigarette shop, our young man came across an old friend in the university, who graduated in agriculture and was now posted to the village as an Asst. Agricultural officer. Whenever our young man met him, his friend always used to irk him with his financial troubles. On one such day, the agricultural officer begged our young man to give him at least Rs. 1000/-immediately to come out of the financial hole he was in. Our young man without any thinking gave him Rs. 700/-, which was given to him by his colleague. The money was never returned to him.

One day, his spouse had arrived with bag and baggage and was put up in a house that was previously taken on rent. The house was very old located in the oldest street of the village. It was dark without any ventilation and dingy for lack of maintenance. But, there was no choice left. The house had a high platform in the central room with an open well in the back yard: There was another two room residential apartment upstairs of the house in which a gentleman with two wives both of whom were sisters was residing. It was a pleasant surprise to see that the two sisters lived in harmony with their husband and there seemed to be no shouts or quarrels among them, as loud voices never reached the couple downstairs. In contrast the family life of this couple started with suspicion. His spouse had brought with her some cooking utensils, an old mat and an old gas stove, which was gifted to her by her aunt. The gas stove was found to be not working. On close scrutiny, it was observed that the plastic pipe leading the gas from the cylinder to the gas stove was split at one place causing the gas to leek at that point. His wife immediately got suspicious of our young man and accused him for the split in the plastic pipe as our young man had commented on the old age of the stove previously. It was the indication of the things to come by. She was educated up to 3rd standard and was not adept in cultivating strangers. Her suspicions about him on the very first day of family life might have sprung up mainly because of two reasons. Firstly, our young man had learnt after the marriage that even though his image was projected in dark light by his relatives and some people of his village, his father-in-law for some reason that might be mainly related to his daughter had decided to give the hand of his youngest daughter to our young man. Secondly, for some unconscious reasons, a trace of abhorrence by him towards her because of her clumsy ways of doing any work and to some extent because of her physical appearance, he had not made any moves after the first night of their marriage to sleep with her. Of course, she, being a shy village girl with little education did not make any moves as natural in this country. She had not brought with her their male child of 8 months old which she should have brought at least for company and playing with him to pass off time. She frequently started complaining about the house. Our young man used to sleep on the platform while his wife used to sleep on the mat spread on the ground. Her complaints might be justified to some extent as pieces of material of the middle layer of the house used to fall on the ground and at any time a scorpion might fall anywhere. She thus stayed for one month and went away to her home sighting the house as the cause of her discomfort.

He had stayed thus in the village for about six months. One day, his head had revealed to him to his utter relief that one of the posts of section officers in divisional office had fallen vacant and enquired whether he was willing to join there. Our young man accepted the offer without any hesitation. The divisional office was located in the town, which happened to be headquarters of the district.

In passing, it might not be inappropriate to have a lucid picture of this gentleman who had been his head for 8 months. He was a peculiar man the likes of whom our young man had come across for the first time. He was a short, plump man of robust health wearing thick glass spectacles. He was aged about 42 years who often had a smile on lips and can bear any kind of insult when money mattered because he was utterly corrupt. He had already had some official allegations against him and was temporarily barred from postings to construction works. He used to deal with each of his sub-ordinates differently depending upon their usage to him. Mainly, he depended on one section officer who was as much efficient as he was corrupt. Even then, this Section Officer he never lagged behind his other colleagues in hurling accusations against the head. Often, this section officer chided his head in front of other technical staff without a whimper of protest from him. He generally never interfered with the daily chores of our young man and talked to him politely. He was stern and arrogant towards others of his sub-division who were inept and did not satisfy his needs. The pride in a man generally changes shades from very light to very dark Vis-à-vis the person being dealt with and the environment surrounding him. It is no secret that a highly successful man reveals this hidden quality discretely while others like the head of our young man manages to achieve their desired goals by exhibiting false pride, as they do not have any worthwhile qualities to be proud of.

The divisional office was located on the outskirts of the town in a recently constructed building. There were two posts for section officers in the division whose main duties were to check the estimates of structures sent by the sub-divisions. Initially, the work was very interesting to our young man because of the simple reason that he excelled on critical assessment of the given issue dissecting it to its bone. Consequently, the staff of the sub-divisions had become more alert in their work and more careful and sensible while manipulating estimates and were prompt in submission.

The divisional officer was a happy man. The divisional officer was fair skinned of medium height bearing aristocratic looks. He came from a highly educated family. Everyone in his division feared him for his commanding and no-nonsense nature. But, he had a weakness of stammering which he tried to conceal to his best of the abilities without positive result. As a result, he spoke very little and that too in brief spells only when it was absolutely essential.

A typical example of the clumsy way of manipulation was best illustrated by the following example.

There were number of open dug wells in both village and agricultural fields as drinking water needs and agricultural activities in these parts mainly depended upon the rainfall and ground water. The young man during scrutiny had come across an estimate of open dug well said to be 50' deep. The water level in the well at the time of inspection was shown as 30' below ground level. Steining of the well was shown up to 20' in the well below ground level, where soils were classified as red earth. From 20' to 30' below ground level, the soils were classified as fractured and fissured rock. From this level up to bottom of the well, the soils were classified as hard rock, which fetches maximum value. They must have classified the soils thus on the presumption that no body in the higher posts could be able to check classification of soils below water and they would just check it on the face value. Our young man naturally posed the obvious question as to how the soils that could not be observed by the naked eye from above could be classified. And, no provision was made in the estimate for dewatering of the well for which the farmers anyhow would not have agreed.

Our young man with the advice of the divisional officer had brought the whole estimating process to a standard pattern and format. The whole exercise was over and the young man heaved a sigh of relief. Suddenly, the Govt. under pressure from affected people had decided that the detailed estimating of the entire house costing more than Rs. 10,000/-had to be done also. So, the gamut of the process had to be repeated. Our young man was not interested in doing such work that had become routine now and applied for transfer to the design unit of the project, which was located at the project site itself.

Mean while we would have a peep into his personal life during his brief stay in the town.

He rented a room near to his office, which was on the outskirts of the town. As he was busy in office form 10 a.m. to 6 p.m., the evening hours were partly spent by taking a walk to the hotel for dinner and chitchatting with his bachelor colleagues working in the other office of the same unit.

One night, he slept in his room without closing the main door. When he woke up in the morning he found some of his possessions such as transistor radio, wristwatch and some clothes were missing from the room. On the advice of some of the office staff, he had given a complaint of theft in the nearby police station. The sub-inspector had visited his room at about 11.00 a.m. and examined the surroundings of the house. He observed some workers engaged in construction work of buildings were residing in a partly completed house. With this observation in mind, he politely enquired our young man whether he was suspicious of any body for the crime. Knowing fully well of what the intentions of the sub-inspector were, he informed the police officer he had none in his mind. The police officer glanced at him with a grin and left the place without bothering to enquire any further. The stolen articles had not been traced and the case had been closed after some months. This incident, unwittingly, would be going to help him immensely in future course of a protest staged by him.

This part of the state was draught prone as the agricultural activities depended upon the scanty and untimely rainfall and un-reliable ground water.

This time of the period, the area was severely draught stricken for the lack of sufficient rain for the past two years. The film actors started on a campaign throughout the state to collect friends for the draught stricken people of the area.

One day, they arrived at the town and were to travel in a procession through the main lanes of the town to collect funds. Our young man with some of his colleagues had taken places at a vintage point on one side of the main market road and was waiting for the film actors to arrive. After about half an hour of waiting the head of the procession came into their sight. Both sides of the lane were filled with enthusiastic people. At the head of the procession, the two big heroes of the silver screen sat on two elephants, which were decorated heavily, one elephant followed by the second. Three open trucks followed the elephants one by one in a row. They were all in slow motion. Two of these trucks were filled up with male actors and the third truck had in it the glamorous female actors of the silver screen. Some actors were walking on either side of the procession with open bags requesting for funds of whatever kind they deemed fit to help the people. The procession stopped for a few minutes at the nearby junction. Suddenly, it was announced on the microphone that any body could shake hands once with any of the actresses by donating one rupee. In the initial seconds there was hesitancy on the part of the people to make a move. All of a sudden, a gentleman started moving towards the truck. Soon, there was a continuous flow of people towards the truck eager to shake hands. It is just for an individual to take initiative for others to follow suit for any cause irrespective of its nature given that wise people participate only in good deeds.

After four months of his stay in the town, a letter arrived from his father-in-law by post informing him that his wife would join him soon. After a long search he could locate a portion of a house suitable for the purpose, which was near to his office. Soon, his spouse arrived with a horde of relatives along with his male child who was then about 1 year old. However, our young man had gone to a cinema theatre as per pre-arranged programme in spite of mild protests from the relatives. On his arrival at the house in the late hours, he saw his son weeping un-controllably because of some discomfort. When he had asked his wife to take care of their son who was in the lap of one of her relatives, she bluntly refused and then there was a commotion. They brought a narrow sleeping cot the bed of which was woven with thick jute threads, which was only adequate for only one person to sleep in comfort. Our young man was very lean and tall man. He could only sleep in the cot by folding his legs. Added to this discomfort, his wife who was very bulky came to join him on the cot. The young man was now really worried as to how he could get at best a nap during that night leave alone a sound sleep. The young man's discomfort reached breaking point when she laid one of her heavy shoulders on his stomach. He immediately got out of the bed in brusque manner and slept on a mat spread on the ground. All the relatives left the place the next day leaving the couple alone. There were frequent skirmishes in the family for one reason or other which were not of any consequence. However, the cause of apparent strain between them was the taste of food prepared by her, which was always, was to his dislike as he was habituated to north Indian food and she being not habituated to cook anything. One day he lost his temper, left the house, and booked a room in a lodge in the town. However, apprehensions of impeding trouble were growing in the minds of his spouse and in laws for the obvious reason which was not justifiable keeping in view of the personality of our young man completely unknown to them. Soon, her father with his sons arrived to persuade him but were bluntly told to first train her in house hold chores.

The term of the then legislative assembly was coming to an end and fresh elections to the state legislative assembly were announced.

Our young man was also drafted as presiding officer to one of the polling stations located about 40 km from the town of a nearby constituency reserved for scheduled castes. Most of the presiding officers drafted for the duty in this constituency were experienced in this exercise except a few like our young man who were recruited for the first time for such a job. The election officers who were responsible for affective and smooth functioning of the machinery during the process were generally from Revenue Department. The revenue officers warned the presiding officers of the bottlenecks that they might face during the process and of consequences in case of shortcomings. The first time recruiters had taken their warnings to their heart and were already a nervous lot. The experienced ones appeared as though they heard nothing and were normal selves as it was a routine discourse by the election officers before every election so that the presiding officers might not take process lightly, and generally were very cooperative at the end of the whole exercise.

The presiding officers along with assistant presiding officers who, were generally three in number in every polling station were asked to assemble at the distribution center, by 8.00 a.m. of the previous day of the scheduled election date, so as to finish the exercise of collection of material by 1.00 p.m., as they have to travel long distances to reach their polling stations. After the tedious work of collection and counting the material issued at several points and comparing the serial numbers of ballot paper and their counting, the batch of our young man were ready to leave for their destination. The farthest polling station of the constituency was about 60 km from the town. These stations were divided into several groups on the basis of the route map of the assembly constituency with a route officer accompanying each group. The polling officers of each group were herded into a waiting open truck parked at a far off point with the polling material in their hands and on their shoulders and were made to stand in the truck till the destination of each group was reached as there were no seating arrangements in the truck. By the time, our young man and his assistants arrived at the polling station which incidentally was located in an elementary school just by the side of the highway avoided further arduous journey with the heavy polling material, it was about 5.00 p.m.

The head of the village had been waiting for them in the school. He was of medium height and well built and might be 45 years old. His eyes were gentle and at the same time sharp enough giving a impression of intelligence that you usually did not find in un-educated village folk. He was very eager to help the polling staff in whatever kind that was desired. Before leaving them to go to village to arrange to prepare food for them, he warned them in a soft voice that this village belonged to the minister of the ruling party who was also now contesting elections and that he brooked no opposition. These words further accentuated the already imbibed tension in them and they were now looking very worried. After the village head left the place, they however turned the attention to complete the formalities necessary for starting poll by 8.00 a.m. next day. There were several envelops with printed proformae to take account of different kinds of ballot papers, like ballot papers for blind and infirm, tendered ballot papers, postal ballot papers etc. Usually, the experienced polling officers virtually ignore them and usually account them as nil. But our presiding officer was determined to follow the procedures in totality. The election started at 8.00 a.m. the next day. In the first two hours, the voting was smooth and peaceful. Suddenly, the presiding officer discovered that one person was trying to accompany the so called blind and infirm people more than once and that some other person was trying to cast his vote more than once impersonating other voters. The presiding officer gently warned them of the consequences of such malpractices and turned them away. After about an hour, a stern looking heavily built man was walking into the polling station. The presiding officer became alert immediately of his intentions and greeted the gentleman with folded hands. This ploy worked and the angry looking man after looking about him for some seconds walked away from the polling station without uttering a word. Within half an hour of appearance of the stranger, a well groomed middle aged woman entered the polling station and tried to accompany the so called blind and infirm voters more than once. When the presiding officer objected to this illegal practice, the lady informed him that she was well aware of the rules and regulations and need not be taught by someone like him and added that these practices were going on in other polling stations also. But the presiding officer stood firm. She was not courageous and rude enough to continue to indulge in these practices and walked away from the station. Later on, the presiding officer came to know that the stern looking stranger was the brother-in-law of the contesting minister and the well-groomed lady was the wife of the minister. But in the confusion arising out of these irksome situations, he forgot to get the signatures of some of the accompanying persons in the performae, which were more than one for this kind of voting. He found the mistake after the stipulated time to cast the votes was over while checking the envelopes. He informed the same to the head of the village who had arrived by then. The head of the village was understanding and kind enough to get the signatures of the concerned.

All work finished and the material packed the polling staff felt immense relief and for the first time were cutting jokes. They were waiting for the truck to take them to the collection center.

But, this was not end of it as far as our young man was concerned. He came to learn the next day that he was drafted to the duties of counting of ballot papers that were cast the previous day. However, a presiding officer's job in the counting process was supervision of counting of votes by his assistants who were two in number and the presiding officer was to clarify whenever a doubt arose about the validity of vote either by the counting officers or the polling agents deputed by the political parties. Observing the honesty and sincerity of our presiding officer, the polling agents had left the table after some time saying that it was not necessary to stand by at this table. It was approaching 1.00 p.m., when lunch was served to all the polling staff. The lunch consisted of a single item called "Upma" served in a cup made of vegetable leaves. Even as the staff were getting restless at the paltry amount served to them, as they were supposed to be on duty from 8.00 a.m. till about 8.00 p.m. by which time the counting process might be completed, our young man discovered that a slight foul smell was emitting from the food indicating that the food was prepared the previous day which could also be verified by touching the food with fingers which could clearly discriminate the fresh food from stale food. The young man got angry and declared then and there that no further counting would be carried on at his table till freshly cooked food in sufficient quantity was served. Another polling officer joined to his aid. All others just kept quiet and were carrying on duties. The revenue development officer who was incharge of the operations had called both of them and enquired about their protest. He warned that the stoppage of the counting of votes in midway might warrant stringent punishment under various acts of elections. When informed of the reasons for their protest, he tried to pacify then by informing them that things like that would generally happen in such contingencies and that it was prudent to adjust for one day and asked them to continue their duties. The two young men instead of getting pacified got more furious and threw the food before the revenue officer and continued their protest. Fortunately, the sub-inspector of police, which was in charge of the law and order of this section of counting kept mum and was moving around as though nothing untoward requiring his attention was taking place. The sub-inspector of police was the same person who came for enquiry about the theft in the room of our young man. The revenue officer ordered for the preparation of fresh food and within an hour fresh good was brought and served to all the duty officers.

From the above incidents it could be safely assumed that the young man had not yet deviated from the so-called true path as appealing to him. Unfortunately he tried to impose some virtues, which he thought were necessary, on his wife, leading to a major catastrophe in his life.

As expected, he was transferred to the design unit at the project site. There, he was allotted an old family quarter. The work in the designs unit was quite interesting and stimulating as no routine work was entrusted to him. Even if some routine work was entrusted to him, he had brought to it more refinement by making suitable suggestions.

After about one year of his arrival at his new working place, his wife returned back to him along with a close relative, who left the next day, and their son who was then 2 years old. The child was a sweet boy bubbling with enthusiasm and was quite handsome to look at even though the color of the skin was quite dark.

This time there seemed to be no hassles from either side of the couple. She got along well with the ladies of the adjacent houses and everything seemed to be going on smoothly. One day, he received a letter by post informing him that his sister and brother-in-law had arrived in the capital of the state and were eager to meet him. He informed his wife and son about his sister's arrival and told them that he would soon go to meet his sister. She made no objection and the son had a list of gifts to be brought from the capital and was looking forward for the day with high expectations. However, his wife asked for nothing to be brought from the city. The next morning, he left the house with a small suitcase, informing them about his departure, and boarded the shuttle bus, which shuttles between the two colonies on the right and left bank of the river, the right bank colony being the main nerve center of activities. The bus stop was only about 100 yards away from his home. He sat in a seat by the window side and was observing the passerby and surroundings as his wont. Suddenly, he caught a glimpse of a woman with hair completely dishevled was walking fast with big strides. Soon, he recognized her as his wife who seemed to be in complete rage. She also boarded the bus and informed him in chocked voice that she was also coming with him to the city. He was severely jolted from his pre-occupation and completely dazed with the sudden development. He soon realized that the situation was very awkward and un-becoming of his position in the locality and got down from the bus and sped to his house and entered a room and bolted from inside. The entire day and night passed quietly even though he had to keep himself hungry with nobody caring to offer him food. In the next morning, to his surprise, he heard footsteps entering his home and he recognized them as his brother-in-law and nephew after hearing their voices. They started abusing his son with an intention of provoking our young man. After some time, our young man came out of his room and asked them to leave.

Immediately, they started beating our young man and had thrown him out of the house. Beaten and bruised, out young man met one of his colleagues in his house, as the office hours had not yet started. He told him about the incident and took some money from him as a loan. In spite of his colleague's requests to stay on to sort out things, our young man shocked and bewildered by the incident, could not remain in the locality a

moment longer. He soon got hold of another shuttle bus to reach the district bus stand on the right bank and left for the city.

CHAPTER 4

1979-1986

After the incident, he reached the city and went to the house off his uncle who was then employed there. He narrated the whole incident to him and informed that he would never go back to that place. All his clothes and other necessary articles of daily usage had been kept in the house at the project site. He knew that his classmate in the high school reside in the city. But, he did not know his address and was not aware whether he used a telephone in his home. He turned the pages telephone directory and several names of his namesake with the same first initial of his surname were marked with a pencil. After several names, which were located in wealthy areas, had been deleted, he could prepare a list of ten names, which needed enquiry, so as to ascertain, the correct Ph.NO. of his friend.

He telephoned these people one by one and at last could locate the house of his friend and thus got the address of his friend. He then went to the residence of his classmate in the earlier years of education, and after narrating the entire episode, had requested him to bring the articles. His friend obliged him immediately and brought all his articles except the furniture and books. His friend informed him that no one was present at his home and all had gone to their native place after locking the door and he could get the key to the lock with great difficulty. He also informed that they before leaving the place made hue and cry and vowed to make him pay for the happenings. After one month, he went to his old station. All the left over furniture was taken out and kept in a friend's home, which he never bothered to take back.

There was a talk in the air that his in-laws were contemplating to lodge a petition in the court of 1st class judicial Magistrate in the town near their place for judicial separation and a civil suit in the court of sub-ordinate judge for division of his ancestral property. One day he received summons from both courts. He went immediately to his native village which was not far from the town, between which the village of his in-laws fell, An aged lawyer of about 60years, who respect old values, was entrusted to fight the semi criminal case and a highly reputed lawyer was engaged to fight the civil suit.

While preparing the counter affidavit before criminal court, differences arose between the lawyer and the younger man. Our young man wanted everything that happened during the day in affidavit for which the wise man disagreed because of his experience in such matters. However, the senior lawyer had to submit to the wishes of the young man who was persistent in mentioning all the facts in the counter affidavit. The young man did not know then that his case was weekend because of his stoic stand. The case was adjourned repeatedly for over one year. Our young man had to attend to the court at least once in every month.

Meanwhile, the young man got himself posted to one of the offices of the department in the city after sustained efforts with the help of his uncle. The unit to which he was now posted deals with the maintenance of the drains in the state in the course of which estimates and tenders were to be approved by his office for carrying out repairs such as removal of vegetation and silt deposited in the drains. It might not be out of place to know something about the Asst. Engineer in charge of the sub division of our young man. Even though he also took bribes for hastening the process of works, he tried to be honest on paper and tried to accomplish the work to the best of his abilities. He was lame, and he walked with some difficulty without any support. He was permitted to work in the offices till his retirement. He was vastly experienced in the office work. Even though all other section officers in his section were considered to be competent and efficient including the predecessor of our young man, their scrutinizing abilities could not be matched by the clinical efficiency with which our man approached any given work. Naturally problems arose. Gradually his officer became a nervous man and unfortunately one day he had a mild stroke and had been bed ridden for a few days. He a kind of abhorrence towards our man. One day, he shouted at our man for some non-existent mistake that the young man was supposedly committed. Our man shouted at him back and that was last time that the both talked to each other. Here, it is to be mentioned that a tinge of recklessness and carelessness regarding his well-being was creeping in to the brain of our young man which was quite natural for a man of his physiology and character as we had already seen.

The tiff between the two soon reached the ears of divisional officer and without any second thoughts our young man was un-scrupulously transferred to the designs section of the same unit. It was not difficult to imagine the mental state of such a person who was beaten up and dragged to court and made to stand in the enclosure as a criminal with stupendous allegations. When he first entered the premises of the court, he appeared to be totally dazed and everything around him looked hazy to his eyes. Most of the time his eyes were focused on the ground and ears focused to hear that one voice that loudly called the names of the persons to enter into enclosure as the turn of their case approached either for arguments or for adjournment depending upon the age of the case. When he entered the enclosure, he seemed to be looking particularly at no one. Though his wife and his son along with her father also attended the court regularly, he never noticed them. After many years, there was a complaint from his son that even though he tried many times to get nearer to his father; he could not to do so for the lack of response from his father.

A man who stood for some virtues had been dragged to court, by the quirk of fate. The funny thing or tragedy about him, even in his present condition, was that he still felt superior to all others in the court including the magistrate who would decide the case and the opposing lawyer he would strive to nail him. Instead of pleading for justice, he looked at them with disdain and contempt. He specially reserved his scornful looks for lawyers of his wife.

The case in the court of magistrate came to hearing, at last, after one year of adjournments. Meanwhile, the relations between our young man and his old lawyer continued to be in friction and the young man dropped him as his counsel and brought a lawyer from the city. This was another mistake he had committed because of which he lost credibility before the magistrate. The charges made against our young man by the complaint could be simplified as:

1) He is a drunkard
2) He beats his wife often
3) He has kept another woman at his previous station.

Our young man was of the thinking that these charges could not be proved in a court of law and the petition of complainant would be squashed.

But, he was in for a shock during the course of the proceeding. The lawyer of his spouse produced an inland letter posted by him to his in laws at the beginning of his service. In the letter, he had requested his father-in-law to send his wife immediately. The lather laced with pungent words indicated that his wife was not interested in leading family life and that she was only habituated to eat and sleep. There was a trace of threat as well in the letter in case of disobedience. As it was the habit of villagers to keep all incoming letters tagged to a wire, they might have, as habit, also kept this letter tagged to the wire probably with no ulterior motives. He prayed to god that an un-intentional safe custody of the letter had to be true. As, otherwise, his mind would not be able to take the jolt of ulterior motives on their part from the very beginning. The lawyer also produced a telegram supposedly sent by his spouse to her father from the previous station, which warned her father about the danger to her life. The result of the case was obvious to everyone. The court believed her and did not trust our young man. Judicial separation was granted.

During the course of the proceedings several attempts had been made to settle the issue amicably out of court. But the in laws were least interested in such proposition knowing fully well that they would win the case. When he lost the case, he engaged lawyer politician from another town to pursue the case further. He also tried to settle the case outside courts and at last his lawyer succeeded in convincing the lawyer of his wife at the discussions held at the lawyer's office when suddenly the lawyer of his spouse desired to see the agricultural lands of our young man inherited from his father, looking particularly at no one. Our over enthusiastic young man immediately informed the lawyer that he was ready to take them to the fields. The young man's lawyer felt insulted at this slip of tongue and walked away from the proceedings. His lawyer also shrugged it off with his inability to proceed further.

Mean while, there was a talk in the air that his in laws were threatening to destroy him and divorce would not be granted to him.

A settlement with in-laws had become all the more important. He renewed his efforts with vigor. He was irregular in sending monthly maintenance allowance to his spouse. A nephew of her, who was a kind gentleman and who resided in the city had consented with our young man that it was better to have a permanent solution to the tangle and agreed to be the mediator. They were able to arrive at a permanent settlement. The settlement in brief was to leave his agricultural land to his wife and treat the returns as annual maintenance, and to give Rs. 10,000/-in cash. The pending issue that was constantly pricking him like a nail in the leg had been settled. That was enough of for him to be free all sorts of tentacles.

Now, it has been about four years since he joined the department. All these years he was pro-occupied either with the office work or family problems. Even though, there was nagging uneasiness of not yet getting divorce, his mind had gone again into its old self as the work in the present office did not need much of his attention. He got divorce papers shortly after wards.

One day while standing in a bus stand, a thought flashed though his mind of what happens to the vast knowledge that is imbibed in the mind of a human being. The answer that had immediately came to his mind was that the soul was nothing but knowledge and that the soul was further evolution of human being. If the theory of gradual evolution of the man being enunciated by Darwin was further taken into metaphysical world, he thought that the God, as we daily define through religions, was nothing but gradual evolution of human being the intermediate being the soul. The moment he thought nay realized that this line of process of thinking would solve various puzzles facing him over the years, he felt un-consciously that he was blessed with some extra-ordinary and un-natural powers. This feeling had stopped his further probing into metaphysical world for a long time for the reasons that would come forth shortly.

The feeling was that he was the supreme commander of elements of earth 'i.e' air, fire, water, earth (human beings) and sky (soul).

Now, he was eager to test his hypothetical powers.

Soon, he got an opportunity in the form of a live cricket match, which was a final of 3rdworld cup being held in England. The final was between the most powerful cricket country in the world at that time and the minnows of cricket. No body gave chance to the minnows to win the cup. As if though proving the predictions of the experts, the underrated country was all-out for 183 runs as they elected to bat first after winning the toss. Now, it was the turn of the champions to bat and to get the required runs as quickly as possible, who had won the last two editions of the world cup. Our young man thought of various options to submit the champions to their first ever defeat in a world cup. He arrived at an option, which he thought was best suited under the prevailing circumstances. He wanted to make use of his powers to make the members of the champion team over confident and reckless in their approach, as the bowlers of the opposing team were not supposed to give them any problem save one all rounder. The champions started their campaign and they were soon 52 runs for 2 wickets and tottering at 66 runs for 4 wickets when the most dangerous batsman of the team had got out of a highly ambitious shot. In no time, the champions were down 6 wickets for 76 runs. It was curtains down for the champion team. Our man could not come to any positive conclusion regarding his powers, as the result might be a coincidence.

Another opportunity soon arrived to test his powers, if any, in the form of a live tennis match in one of the grand slam tournaments. This was a final match between two Americans. One man of the namesake of Courier the other man called Sampras who in those times was ranked no .1 in the world and was considered one of the greatest players of all times. The gap between the skills of the players was so yawning that nobody gave a chance to the other gentleman to win the tournament. The gentleman called Courier was two sets down and lagging behind the champion in the third set by 3 games to 4. Our man thought of various options to achieve his goal and finally decided that the best way under the circumstances was to enthuse him to the maximum possible extent and make him confident that he could still win the match as such results were not uncommon in the game of tennis. The underrated gentleman won the match and the title and climbed to number one spot and continued in that position for few weeks. He still thought it might it be just a coincidence. He was looking for another opportunity to test his powers.

The country was passing through a period of hibernation. The mistrust among people was on the ascendancy. The un-accountability of various institutions was reaching to its peak. The rate of development of the country had come down appreciably save for green revolution and vast strides the dairy cooperatives had taken. Corruption, which was limited to certain privileged strata of the society till then, had now become the pre-occupation of everybody that mattered in the society. Under such scenario, the head of government of a state had been overthrown with the connivance of the central command. The drama that preceded the downfall was not only breathtaking but also credible which sustained the faith of the people in democracy and sincerity of purpose and honesty in dealings.

Our man came to the conclusion that because of the leader of the country, the politics of the country and administration of the country were losing credibility among people and hence should be removed from the sphere of the activity. He had now begun to think of the way, which was most suitable and effective for achieving the result. Unknown faces on one minority community were kept still in his frame of mind and were ordered to remove the leader from the scene of life. By moving his index finger with his eyes closed on a calendar, he arrived at a date and month of the current year by which time the mission would be accomplished. Soon, he forgot the entire mission.

On one particular day, which was the deadline set, while he was in office, news broke out about the assassination of the leader, which pierced through his ears like the sound of a bomb exploded nearby. He was momentarily dumb founded but regained senses quickly to learn more about the assassination. He was still not sure of his powers. This might be another coincidence. He had been transferred to another unit dealing with designs after his term of 10 years in the previous unit.

He joined the new post and started working as vigorously as he always did in his official duties. Once, while checking the salient features of a multistoried building to be constructed for the department, it was observed by him that the total plinth area for which the architect had furnished the drawings based on which the designs were underway, was exceeding the plinth area actually permitted by the Govt., The discrepancy was brought to the notice of one his colleagues. He than brought it to notice of the officer who was actually responsible for this verification before our man came into picture. His colleague told him that if the above fact were revealed to any third person, our man would face dire consequences. This man here afterwards called Mr. X was highly resourceful and was very close to the head of the unit and was to get promotion shortly. In spite of all this, our man had put up detailed office note describing about the discrepancy among other features, to his higher officer. The file was kept lying on the table without any action.

When one day, he entered the office as usual, atmosphere around him appeared to be deadly quiet with a feeling of un-earthiness about it. Those officers who had already come were glancing at him curiously. He had gone straight to his seat and sat there uncomfortably. The drawers of his table seemed to have been searched and disturbed, as he never locked them. He did not dare to get up and speak to any of the office staff. After sitting about two hours with discomfort, he left the office without informing anybody with all kinds of thoughts swarming his brain. He boarded a city bus with an uncommon feeling that the passer-by were looking at him curiously. After the bus started for its destination, where the house of man was located, two persons bent slightly towards him making valiant efforts as though sensing something queer. Our man was fully immersed in his own thoughts about what was happening and what might be the causes for all this strange behavior from others. He then gradually began to think of various omissions and commissions he had done during past few years. He remembered that he sold an old Television set to a villager on the behest of his friend whose switches were not working well. The episode of plinth area also came to his mind. Is it to do something with this? He was so confused that a strange fear started building in him. He sat completely immovable till his destination was reached. He disembarked the bus and heaved a huge sigh of relief as though he had just jumped out of the fire safely. But, a sudden sound of hand digging iron instruments thrown to the ground from the bus sent shivers through his spine. He encountered the same peculiar glances as he reached his house.

The moment he entered the house, he broke down under the sudden impact of severe headache piercing his brain from all sides and with a feeling of being pounded on the head with blunt instruments. He now began to look at every person including his wife with suspicion. His mouth has dried up and the glands secreted no saliva. The taste of food seemed to be pungent and created a sensation of omitting. He was unable to eat anything solid except rice mixed with buttermilk that too with much difficulty. He began to smoke cigarettes continuously without a gap to free himself from the mental turmoil he was in of which he was unable to understand anything about it.

His mind had deteriorated so much that he began to presume that even the cigarettes he was smoking might be filled with poison, as their taste was stale as well as acidic to his senses. He became so restless, confused and bewildered by the wayward brain, he was unable to sit at one place for more than few moments and was constantly pacing the rooms and verandah continuously.

And all of a sudden, it occurred to him either by presumption or from circumstantial evidences that everybody around was able to understand of what was going on his mind. This was a terrible shock to him. At the same instant, the un-conscious self asked him chant the name of GOD "OM NAMO NARAYAN" continuously. He than began to chant the above mantra in his mind continuously. All of a sudden, peace and tranquility returned to him.

The atheist might argue that once he concentrated on a thing which does not bring conflict into his thinking and that his mind was focused, state of mind would be peaceful.

Whatever may be the reason, Peace had returned to him and he was continuously chanting the name of God. He then beckoned his family members and asked them to be ready to go to his native place to see his grand parents. He along with his family members went to the central bus station and brought tickets for two as his children were minors of less than 2 years old. He was allotted rear seats of the bus, which were only available. He sat on his seat cross-legged keeping both the hands on the upper leg with one palm over the other. On the left side, his family was seated. On the right side, some strangers were seated. Either accidentally or intentionally, the man by his right side put his leg with shoes on his bare foot. And he was pressing his shoe hard on the foot of our man, our man wished that it was nothing but that of wool and that sensation of softness persisted.

He was at this point was certain that his thinking was understood by everyone around him. After the bus had left the city outskirts, he suddenly ordered that it should rain heavily. Rain started to pour heavily throughout his journey till he reached the town. By the time they reached the town, the rain almost stopped except for occasional drops.

They soon reached the village where his grand parents were presently staying. The moment he entered, all kinds of thoughts mostly fanciful, have again swarmed his mind. For the first time it occurred to him that someday was trying to kill him. Now his eyes were fierce and face reddish with anger. He could not stay much longer there. He walked through the agricultural fields leaving paved road in an angry mood taking large strides. What he did not know was that his family members were also following him in whatever conveyance they could get hold of. Once in the town, he was taken to the house of one of his brother's-in-law. Even now, his mind was in turmoil and in volatile condition and afraid of something of which he had least knowledge. He was so thirsty that in spite of consuming water continuously, the mouth was getting dried as fast as he consumed water.

His restlessness brought him outside the house and he entered the premises of a nearby place of worship. The moment he entered the place, peace seemed to have returned to him, nay, temporarily as one of the priests spat on seeing him disturbing his mind again.

He got out into streets and reached central bus station, and tried to embark a bus bound for the city without ticket. He then got out of the bus and sat on the wide and long foot steps of the entry to the bus station for a while and then straightway walked to a police station near by.

At the police station, he complained that a plot was being hatched to kill him. The police took him along with his relatives in a police van to a private nursing home and joined our man there on the advice of his relatives. This is the last thing he remembered at the end of one month in the hospital.

CHAPTER 5

1986-1996

He was discharged from the hospital after one month's stay. He completely recuperated from the illness. He was now hale and was as normal as he was before getting attacked by that terrible head pain. But the incidents continue to linger his mind and was unable to get over them. After expiry of the leave he resumed his duties at the previous station without any hitch. The monsoon had just set in. Drizzles were common of the day. But alas, quiet and turbulent free life was not for him. His doctor in the hospital had advised him not to wet his head for at least two months. Whenever he used to venture outside during a drizzle, the drizzle used to cease immediately. The incidents like this used to puzzle him and throwing his mind into a whirlpool of thoughts about the unusual incidents that took place during his recent journey. It is here pertinent to know that our man till now had neither divulged to any one the past events of his life nor shared with anyone his thoughts and perceptions about life and god. But the events that had taken place recently were so perplexing that he no longer could sustain the secrecy he maintained till now and he was itching to confide the recent events to someone. But his inner voice seemed to warn him against any divulgence as otherwise immense harm might come to him. However, his mind in the anxiety of unveiling the secrecy could not understand as to how the disclosure might cause him any harm, as also there was every possibility that it might be ignored and treated in a lighter vein on the assumption that it was nothing but an illusion of an unhealthy mind and as such nothing but fictitious imagination. He was unable to perceive the consequences even if anyone were to believe it to be true. His mind was clogged in his anxiety to show off his greatness. He narrated the recent events to his closest acquaintance in the office, who was deeply religious. The man was kind, generous and was considered highly intelligent. This man here afterwards called Mr. Y heard him in rapt attention and withdrew without making any comments. Our man was perplexed by his behavior. One reason for his behavior that flashed through his mind might be the incident that took place in a place of worship which belonged to a minority community.

At this particular point of time, an oil rich nation in the Arab world attacked and occupied a tiny neighboring oil rich country. One of the super powers plunged into the crisis in support of the tiny nation, and warned the attacker of imminent war if it does not withdraw from the occupied territories immediately. Everybody is discussing about imminent war as the attacking country ignored the threats of the super power.

During this period, a book written by a 15th century French astrologer named Nostradamous professing to foretell the future events had come into prominence. The book was being sold like hot cokes. The book was a composition of verses divided into several chapters. An English translation of the verses was also contained in the book. It could be understood from the verses that their nature was general in nature and it was difficult to make head or tail out of them. Most of the verses were mainly about imminent future wars in the various regions of the world. The beauty of the verses was that any body could draw his own desired conclusion without the fear of rejoinder from others.

As the attacking country was diffident, the superpower had started preparations in all earnest to throw out the enemy from the occupied territories. A rumor was gaining ground that according to the predictions of Nostradamus, the super power would be humiliated and defeated in the war. The religious fanatism had risen to such a level that common sense had gone awry and the reality about the immense strength and reach of the super power did not matter. When a discussion on the subject cropped up in the office, our man like every other neutral person had opined that the superpower would annihilate the attacking country within a few days after the start of the war. Mr. 'Y' was not happy with the attitude of our man. The troubles for our man began from then onwards. On the next day, some of his colleagues in the office were glancing at him peculiarly.

It now appeared that Mr. 'Y' confided the entire events to Mr. 'X' for Mr. X was looking at our man with his eyes, which were showing marked signs of abhorrence and his facial muscles suddenly twitched which our man understood as the clear signs of some malevolent intentions. Our man was getting worried. It all started with a slight headache.

As the days were passing by, he was experiencing a kind of swirling pain in his head. After some days, the condition of his brain had become such that as if utter chaos had invaded his brain. His head was experiencing twirling pain. Some people suggested that his condition might be probably due to in adequate circulation of blood in the veins of his brain. He confided his condition to Mr. 'Y' with who he was still in good terms. Mr. 'Y' informed him that he knew a professor of the city university who had magical powers similar to a sorcerer, but not in a strict sense, and heals some kinds of ailments by his unnatural powers with the grace of God. Mr. 'y' advised him to approach the professor and informed him that he would be pleased to take him to the professor. Knowing the history of our man, Mr. 'Y' might have probably given that advice.

One day, Mr. 'Y' took our man to the professor. The professor was simple in his manners and dress and kind looking. He looked like any other man we meet in the streets. The professor beseeched our man to sit in another chair opposite him and pressed his smooth fingers around his forehead moving his fingers all the while along his forehead and seemed to be reciting some divine verses silently. Slowly, the fore head of our man started sweating and soon beads of sweat started flowing down the head on to his neck. Our man felt some semblance of peace and the intensity of pain had somewhat receded, which quantitatively could be assessed to be one fifth of the initial quantum. After half an hour, the professor stopped the process and informed him that it might take several days to completely heal him and that he would have to meet him once in a week on a particular day. The professor resided in a remote and highly congested place far away both from the residence of Mr. 'Y' and the office. Our man did not want to further bother his colleague 'ie' Mr. 'Y' and dropped the idea of meeting the professor for further sittings.

Here, it is important to note that the illness of our man is in no way affecting his ability to carry out his duties in the office. For the reasons not known to him, his colleagues in the office were gradually distancing themselves away from our man. Our man was not sure of the reasons. He was a further disturbed by their behavior. He was not getting sound sleep at nights. However he maintained his mental stability and calmness and tried his best to carry out his duties to the satisfaction of his superiors.

He now consulted a psychiatrist and started medication as advised by him. The doctor was a sturdy old man of about 60 years age with thick long moustaches giving the looks of a stern but respected teacher. The doctor in the initial stages did not use to ask our man any questions and whatever he wanted to know he got it from his wife who always accompanied him to the doctor. The doctor had always had soothing words to say and he used to assure him that he had got the right medicines for whatever ailment that he was suffering from. However, unfortunately this was not the end of road for our man.

Our man was outspoken, frank and straightforward. So, whenever a discussion on any subject took place with his colleagues, the thought that his frank opinions and strait forward and somewhat curt replies might hurt them had not entered his mind. Under the circumstances, this type of his behavior was bound to aggravate his problems, as we would see in due course of time.

Because of the strong dosage of medicines he was taking, he was feeling physically very weak and his mind was getting numb. Suddenly one day, he observed that the persons passing nearby him and passengers in the city bus sitting next to him and his colleagues in the office were glancing at him puzzled and confused. He was beginning to understand that something had gone wrong somewhere. His thinking had become unceassant and at the same time aimless and multi directional. He was now certain that the disease he dreaded most had enveloped him again. That is, everyone who was nearer to him now understood his thought process. It was a terrible feeling to know that others could decipher his thought process. Despite of his best efforts to stop thinking by concentrating on either a single object or a specific subject, he failed in his attempts. So, he gradually developed absurd and haphazard thinking with an intention to confuse others. So even when some past events flashed through his mind, people would not distinguish between truths and false. But, of course with the passage of time, this habit had become another malice. This illness had brought with it a new problem. It appeared to him that one class of people was sympathetic towards him while another class of people was apathetic towards him. The poor class of people appeared to be helping him while the middle class people appeared to be tormenting him. Why this divide ? It would be known later on. Unwittingly, he was drawn into an acute psychic syndrome. Inspite of all this, he still felt that he was an extra-ordinary man with unusual super natural powers which he was not exercising at present.

He frequently suffered from several ailments such as a feeling of gas flowing through his body; inadequate production of saliva and subsequent drying up of month; severe head pain; sudden heating up of the body; constipation; knee pain; acute physical weakness etc. Whenever the nature of any ailment or combination of them was acute, he used to visit his doctor in addition to the regular visits. As usual, he had always had soothing words to say and prescribed medicines, which our man thought, had acted as a temporary deterrent. Additionally, whenever his ailments were grave there usually used to be a heavy downpour of rain, which further reduced the intensity of the ailments. During the months of summer, he had to be extra careful because of the natural heat. During summer months, his wife used to go to his elder sister's house in the town far away from the city. During one such month of a summer, I narrate the following incidents that took place, which led him to a state of mind that may precede the beginning of the insanity conditions in a human being.

On a public holiday, while he was walking to his house from the bus stand, some persons coming opposite to him were spitting before him probably out of disgust and some other persons were looking at him in anger. He went straight to his house with his head bowed to avoid views around him and switched on the T.V to ward of the swirling thoughts of about the past happenings especially of what he all along presumed that he was instrumental in the killing of a national leader and was often presumed to have been conveyed to the people through his thought process. This sudden thought flashing through his mind unnerved him completely. Suddenly he was afraid that some body was trying to kill them. He furiously walked to and fro in the rooms of his house and after some time had tried to concentrate on what was happening on the T.V screen. As night approached, he consumed the medicines as usual and lay down on the bed awaiting sleep to overtake his thoughts. After about two hours, instead of the approach of sleep, sounds of beating of drums reached his eardrums. He thought that certain section of people was celebrating his impeding death. As night passed, the sounds became louder to him. But he had not dared to get up from the bed and to go outside to verify. Actually, this was all his illusion. It he was to open the eyes and come outside, he would not have heard any sounds. Some how, he spent the night and heaved a huge sigh of relief, which was only momentary, at the advent of the dawn. After some how completing the early morning chores, he had gone out nervously to have breakfast. It appeared to him that a kind of threatening silence had prevailed all around him. The loneliness, was all the more suffocating. He had decided to go to the house of one of his acquaintances. He had hired an auto and approached his house. He called for him several times from the gate of his house without any response. The gate was locked from inside. As there was no response, he scaled the small compound wall only to find that the door was also locked. He thought that they had left the house only to avoid meeting him. He straightway went to the railway station and awaited for the train which would take him to the town to where his wife had gone. At the same time he was looking around whether any body had been following him. The waiting, which seemed unending was at last over and the train steamed on to the platform. He entered a general compartment and sat on a seat by the side of the entrance gate. After few minutes, he observed that four hefty men embarked the same compartment. He thought that they were following him. By afternoon, the train reached the destination point. He then went to the city bus stop and looked around to know whether any body had been following him. After satisfying that no one was following him, he embarked a city bus in a relaxed mood. The bus was bound to go in the same route in which the house of his sister-in-law was located. As the bus started, a whiff of fresh air gushed through the window. Here an unnatural thing happened. He inadventarily thought that the fragrance of various flowers should envelop the bus. Suddenly, he could smell the fragrance of jasmine and then the fragrance of rose flowers and he thought that the passengers of the bus were also experiencing the same thing. But, the faces of the passengers were nonchalant and he could find no trace of surprise on the faces of any of the passengers. At that time, he remembered that his doctor once enquired him whether he was experiencing any kind of smells and sounds in his cars. He now became completely relaxed and entered the house of his sister-in-law and fell at ease.

The emission of sonic waves from his head according to his perception generally lasts only for few days. But once, the melody persisted for long and he became a worried man. He had become highly depressed. The state of high depression was as dangerous as any other dangerous disease. His psychiatrist advised him to consult a general physician. The general physician got conducted all the tests that he felt necessary and finally concluded that there was nothing wrong with his physical system and was only suffering from acute depression which he had to overcome by his own will power.

On one of those days, he met his uncle and he advised our man to approach certain occultist cum ayurvedic doctor. Our man enquired about the doctor and learned that he was a highly respected gentleman in the society and was revered by his followers. As advised, one day he reached his clinic along with one of his relatives at about 5.00 AM in the early morning. Already, there was a long queue of patients. He stood in the queue for about two hours. At about 7.00 AM, a young man came and collected Rs. 60/.-from each of the patients and then gave each of them a metal token with an inscribed serial number. On enquiry, he was informed that his turn to meet the doctor could come at about 2.00 pm in the evening. There was a shrine of a saint in front of the clinic among beautiful surroundings. They took some refreshments and had a darshan of the saint and spent some time in the shrine. A beautifully carved marble statue of life size stood in all its grandeur in the centre of a big hall with white marble flooring. At about 1.00 PM, they entered the clinic which had a large hall with wooden benches here and there. As the benches were fully occupied, they had to wait standing. After about two hours, his number was called and he was beckoned towards a young man sitting beside a tiny wooden table. He was given a paper with printed matter on it after his name was entered in a register. He filled up the blanks on the paper and was dumbfounded when he read the lines below. There were writhen the names of all species of demons, devils and sprits that he had often heard since his childhood. At last his turn came to meet the occultist. The occultist was a middle-aged man of about 50 years. He was rotund in shape and of small stature with a round face and of very fair complexion. He had a benign smile on his face. He stood inside a room by the side of a long wooden table beautifully carved upon which a large crystal sphere, fixed on a beautifully shaped small steel stand, stood. The room had a wide opening through which he talked with his patients. He glanced at our man with a smile and gazed through the crystal ball for few seconds. He then fell silent for few seconds and then began to cross out all the names of demons and devils printed on the paper, which our man had already handed over to him. He then called one of his assistants and commanded him to call our man the next morning to the clinic and to wash his naked body with water and to place a seed of a particular species in a tray of soils and to pour some of the washed water into the tray. The occultist told our man that he would become all right if the seed germinates by the next morning. Our man never went to the place again. His peculiar ailment was however cured on that day it self.

His life dragged on with frequent disorders as explained in this chapter for six long years. What was more saddening was the attitude of his colleagues and the people in his surroundings majority of whom appeared to have no sympathy for his plight.

On cool contemplation and analyzation of the events during the last six years, he came to the conclusion that medication alone would not cure his ailments and actual cure lied elsewhere. He ultimately zeroed onto two persons who were Mr. 'X' and Mr. 'Y' as the genesis and root cause of all his problems. He then decided to defend himself and to strike back.

One day, he called Mr. X and Mr. Y outside the office and asked them not to continue with those activities that were causing harm to him. Mr. 'Y' replied that he would not do any such things in future while Mr. X feigned complete ignorance. Our man then thought that it was very difficult to deal with Mr. X. He however warned them that he would not keep quiet any longer if they indulge in any untoward activities in future and that they would be in for a shock.

On the next day in the office, he was in the chair and was immersed in his work. Suddenly, his upper lip started quivering mildly. He thought that some untoward malady might strike him soon. He looked around and saw that Mr. Y was with his boss and was getting up to return to his seat. He immediately stood up and started walking towards the direction in which he had to return to his seat. As he approached Mr. Y, he intentionally brushed his shoulder brusquely in full view of the office staff sitting in that part of the big hall, which was divided into two portions. He then saw that the face of Mr. Y was slightly contorted and soon he began to move his mouth in an awkward manner. He stayed in the office for a few minutes and then left the office in utter shock. The glow in the eyes of the officers indicated to him that they did not mind the incident. Mr. Y returned to the office the next day apparently conveying the message that he was normal and feeling fine.

Everything seemed to be normal in the office till the evening. At about 4.00 PM, some staff of the office especially attendants appeared to him to be wiping their eyes. On seeing them, our man understood that something was amiss and waited for any eventuality. He noticed that Mr. Y was not seen in the office after 4.00 PM.

The office closes at 5.00 P.M. At about 5.00 P.M, he got up from his seat and started slowly walking to the bus stop, which was about half KM from the office, brooding about the behavior of the attendants. He waited for the bus to arrive at the stop, which was its starting point. On arrival of the bus after about 15 minutes as per its scheduled time, he boarded the bus and occupied a seat by the side of a window, which was usual place. Soon the bus was filled up. He then observed that dark clouds were gathering in the sky. The bus started on scheduled time and suddenly stopped after covering a distance of about half a kilometer. Now the sky was full of dark clouds and a dark carpet spread the sky hiding the sun completely. Some passengers were looking at him angrily as though he was responsible for the delay. The bus had not started till it started to rain, which was his usual for the bus to stop for there was no apparent mechanic failure. The passengers were dismayed but everybody kept quiet. It started with mild showers and started gradually intensifying. By the time he reached his house, the sky had opened up and there was heavy down pour. As he entered the house, he felt that his whole body was suffering from a peculiar pain like that when it happened when the body was pricked with sharp needles all over. After about half an hour, the pain had completely subsided.

On the next morning, when he went to the office, he observed that the normally docile lift men and attendees had become assertive and a confident lot and looked at him with respect which of course would not last longer than that day. When he returned to his house in the evening, he felt severe body pains all over the body. He waited for about two hours for the pains to subside. As there was no relief, he decided to use his powers, which he thought that he still had. He silently uttered the following words. The supreme commander of the earth command the elements of the earth to teach him a lesson, facial features of whom he had imprinted in his mind. There was a sudden jerk in the body followed by shivering, which lasted for few seconds. His body pains had completely subsided. He thought that from then on wards, no harm would occur to him. But, subsequent unfolding of events proved otherwise.

On the next day in the office, he observed that Mr. X was looking angrily at him and that he had gone out of the office after some time. Mr. Y appeared to be normal but his face was somewhat gloomy. After one hour, he again felt body pains, which surprised him. Now, the pride in him had gone down considerably. He understood that the forces work not only for him but also work for other persons against him with equal intensity unmindful of his wishes. But as time passed by, the intensity of his illnesses were being reduced considerably. And some of the illnesses had vanished.

He also came to understand that any person with hatred and mal-intentions towards him could do no harm by himself, which Mr. X and Mr. Y already knew. As a result, they had approached other members of the staff who were willing to help them. Accordingly, he had to alter his commands with the picture of no particular person in the frame of his mind. He observed that if he were to use his commands on any innocent person, the forces would boomerang on him. So, he had to be more careful and patient.

As the days further passed by, he also observed that any body going outside the office seeking the help of outside agencies could no longer do any harm to him as long as he stayed outside. They, with whatever ailment they had acquired outside, used to come to office after some time and used to sit nearer to him, conveying our man that something was wrong with them. Here, it is pertinent to mention that the mind of our man is highly flexible and it thinks in all angles about the cause of their malady and often used to come to the conclusion that the fault might lie with him only. The moment this thought used to enter his mind, the ailment of other persons used to get transferred to him gradually with in a few minutes, which might not be of the same nature.

Here, I narrate an incident that had occurred in the office on a certain day. One of his colleagues came and sat in the vacant chair beside him and another colleague was already sitting in a chair besides the first colleague on his other side. He observed that the face of the first colleague was covered with moisture with a strange gleam about it and further the face was darker than usual with contracted cheeks. Our man felt that slowly his body was getting heated up. Our man issued his commands. After few seconds, the innocent person sitting besides this person fell unconscious. The commands were so forceful that the heat traveled through the person sitting beside him to the innocent man. The perception of the event was only of our man. Here it is pertinent to mention that no body either from the office or from outside talks to him about these things at any time. So, the mind of our man was always tense not knowing of would happen next.

After two years, Mr. X and Mr. Y were transferred on promotion and posted to places far away from the city. Our man heaved a huge sigh of relief. The problems for him gradually subsided. Except for some side effects of the medicines he was consuming, he almost became normal. Consequently, the medication was gradually reduced. After one year, he was also transferred from the place on promotion to a town far away from the city. He then used to visit his doctor in the city once in a month. After one year, the doctor prescribed him a single tablet of minimum possible strength, which he had to consume once every day during night continuously with out any break. The doctor also informed him there was no necessity for our man to visit him again in future as he was almost cured.

Here it is important to mention that our man has arrived at a theory that God was nothing but further evolution of human being as already mentioned. From then onwards, he was trapped by the forces that he thought to have acquired and was plunged into such a crisis all through these years that his thinking was entirely revolved around his health and was limited to the extent of saving himself from purported outside forces.

He at last realized that the powers hampered his progress and his thinking process had not evolved beyond that and he had been almost thrown into abysmal depths. He ultimately proclaimed within himself that he at once deserted all the powers that he thought he had. It is also important to note here that Mr. Y has met him accidentally after four years at the head quarters of the department, and during course of his talk, he informed our man that he had suffered, during those turbulent times, a lot more than our man. However, at the time of the meeting, he appeared robust, healthy and highly energetic. He also informed him that he had a presentation about his project before the principal secretary and seemed highly enthusiastic about it.

However, our man has kept himself engaged only to the meager work he had on hand at the new station. His thinking had never gone beyond the work and other mundane matters. After a quiet life he had at the new station for three years, he got himself transferred again to the city because of some family constraints.

CHAPTER 6

1996-2002

Degeneration of values had become more widespread in the social system consequent to deterioration and weakening of political system and its telling effect on the functioning of the Government system. Presently setting aside other harmful qualities of human being which have been there in some mundane from or other from time immemorial, we now deal with briefly the genesis of corruption in modern India (The independent India) and its envelopment of the whole society to such an extent that it was now considered as an unavoidable evil and had come to be accepted by the majority of the society as un-avoidable evil and part and parcel of daily life. This country is considered as one of the most corrupt countries in the world. Corruption makes in-eligible and evil persons richer and stronger.

To find the genesis of corruption in independent India, let us go back to its initial years. It could have been started as harmless bribery indulged by the low paid employees of the Government at the bottom of its hierarchy, like bribe taken to get certificates attested by gazetted officers and to hasten the procedure involved in getting things done. The payment system of British Government was such that the natives at lower and middle level were paid meager salaries, which were continued after independence. After some years, when the political bosses began to give more importance to their workers, sycophants could have crept into systems at this juncture and could have started getting small favors from their bosses probably out of compassion aroused because of the poverty of the sycophants. Then, the alteration of norms and guidelines could have been started at the middle level of Govt. system to suit the political sycophants, as no common man would dare to alter the existing system. Sycophancy has been prevalent in India from time immemorial. It was imbedded in the religion of the region. Once a seed was placed, it is bound to germinate and grow on to become a mammoth tree. As years passed by, the strength of sycophants had increased.

Gradually, the almost mono political system has become a week multi party political system. Now, a new breed of muscle men could have seeped into the political system making a mockery of the Govt. system. Another and more dangerous breed of manipulators gained importance in the scheme of things and all these three together had enveloped the political system as the political bosses fight for their survival. The bureaucracy had become docile to the political system for its survival. Why and how an independent India founded on the principles of non violence and truth had gone into the hands of a political system which comprised persons on most of whom an average Indian had lost faith?. Is it because of social structure in which there was an alarming gap between rich and poor and literate and illiterate in which the majority were poor and illiterate?

Now, coming to the other harmful qualities of human being such as greed, lust, jealousy, violence etc. From whence these qualities seeped into the minds of human beings or what were the reasons for the development of these qualities in human beings? The genesis of all the evils imbibed in a human mind could be traced to hunger, sex and intelligence and the human being started to crave for enjoyment while mitigating hunger and sex contrary to the animals resulting in these evils more pronounced in human beings. A man could not be found fault with for having these qualities which were there in nature in every creature but the difference being that the higher level of intelligence the human being was blessed with by the Creator.

The nature and the universe and all kinds of matter including human beings were because of the creator, the ultimate power. Creator is creation itself. The relationship between the creator and creation can be best explained by the big bang theory which professes that the entire universe is caused and gradually developed because of splitting open of a single point of infinite density and strength. Hence, creator exists in every substance of creation. Here, I distinguish between God and Creator, God being the gradual evolution of human being. As such God is also part and parcel of creation. A special quality that is given to human mind is rationalism, that is the ability of human being to rationalize things.

Hunger and sex brought forth violence, greed, lust and jealousy among creatures. But in human beings, hunger and sex coupled with gradual development of intelligence to dizzy heights, brought forth many other evils. The basic evils were compounded and multiplied into multitude of evils, the impediment to their spread being the rationalism. Here comes the importance of a rational law and order system which had to be implemented strictly and neutrally for the society to move forward smoothly to a truly rational system. Here, the question that normally arises was why the law and order system that ran almost smoothly in developed countries, had so many bottlenecks in developing and poor countries. Is then the poverty and illiteracy the root cause for the in-effective implementation of law and order system in these countries and founding of irrational law and order system in some countries? Many religions had come into existence. Many saints had come and gone. Is there any change in the general attitude of human being?

Here, I narrate an incident, which took place while our man was working in the town, this incident might throw some light on the working of law and order system.

While being almost one year into his service in the town, one day our man and one of his juniors were assigned a job of being witnesses to an operation carried out by anti corruption bureau. They were simply ordered to go to a certain room in the guesthouse of their project located nearby the office where the officers from A.C.B had been waiting for them. They were told nothing more than that. On entering the room they found that six persons were seated in cane chairs and on cots. They learned that of these, four belong to A.C.B and the other two were complainers. The raiding party consisted of a Dy. Superintendent of police, one officer of the rank of Inspector, one sub-inspector and a constable. The head of the raiding party was approaching his fifties and was an amicable and easygoing gentleman. The other officers were somewhat aloof and stern looking. The complainers were young in their thirties and were nervous in their demeanors. They introduced themselves to our officers. Then, the officer-in-charge explained about the operation to be carried and sternly warned our officers not to leave contact with them till the operation was over next day and to keep the operation a complete secret till it is completed. The operation was about catching a sub-inspector of police of the town police station red handed while taking bribe from the complainers.

The methodology of operation was discussed thread bare and was finalized suitable to the surroundings of the house and the time of the arrival of the sub-inspector to his house which would be generally about 8.00 pm in the evening. For the past four days, an officer of A.C.B had been observing the movements of the S.I and his routine schedule. During the previous day, another officer of A.C.B. thoroughly surveyed the surroundings of the house and enquiries were made about his neighbors pretending himself as a census officer.

The modus operandi is as detailed bellow.

Two police officers would post themselves about 100' from the house at strategic places. One officer would be placed him self about 20' away from them on the other side of the crossing of the main road with the street road in which the house was located. The complainers would be wandering about cross roads till the approaching time of S.I. Then they would be posted themselves in a dark place by the side of a provisions shop. The remaining two officers including the in charge and our two officers would be seated in the jeep which would be parked in an alley from which place the crossing of the street road with the main road could be observed and was not more than 50' from the crossing. On the arrival of S.I. on his motorbike at the crossing, the officer near to the crossing that is in front of the general stores would signal the complainers to proceed to the house of the S.I. The complainers were given a small torchlight. If they are successful in bribing the S.I, one of the complainers would casually walk out of the house and would give two signals by switching on the torchlight twice which would be visible to the two police officers who would then rush towards the building to catch hold the S.I. red handed.

After explaining the modus operandi, one of the officers of A.C.B had shown to our Govt. officers a bottle of chemical powder and explained about its usage. The chemical powder would be sprinkled on the currency notes. When these sprinkled currency notes or any matter sprinkled with the chemical powder was immersed in water, the water would turn pink in colour. Then the numbers of currency notes brought by the complainers which consist of two bundles of Rs. 100' denomination were noted on a white paper and authenticated by the Govt. officers. Then the chemical powder was sprinkled on the bundles. The sprinkled powder was how ever invisible to the naked eye.

At 7.30 pm, the party left the guesthouse and reached the place of operation by 7.40 pm. The officers posted themselves at the pre-determined spots, and the complainers started walking to and fro nearby the third officer. At about 8.10PM, the S.I reached the crossing and straightway went to his home. The complainers immediately followed him to his house. After about 10minutes, the officers in the jeep heard shouts and then thumping of boots and it was observed that the three police officers were running towards the house of the S.I Our officers and the in charge on reaching the house learnt that the S.I smelt something wrong and ran away from the house after accepting the bribe before the A.C.B could reach him. The officers of A.C.B ran after him and caught him in a house 200' away. By the time the A.C.B caught the S.I, the currency notes had vanished. It was learnt that this house belonged to a nephew of the S.I and the nephew who was a constable was absconding. The S.I was brought to his house and both the houses were searched thread bare without any success.

However, a handkerchief was found in one of the pockets of the trouser the S.I was wearing. The water turned pink when the handkerchief was immersed in the water to the great relief of all concerned. The S.I in spite of being threatened did not accept his guilt. Then an inventory of all the articles in the house was prepared and was authenticated by the government officers. The handkerchief was placed in a pocket made of cloth and was sealed along with the water bottle of pinkish water. The operation lasted the whole night.

After about 1-½ years, a notice had reached our man and his junior ordering them to be present before a judge of the special court of the A.C.B in the city on a certain date. Now, important and highly placed politicians had started calling our man on telephone with a request to present his evidence in favor of the half trapped sub-inspector. The sub-inspector himself met our man twice to help him. Our man expressed his in ability to twist the evidence as the evidences were already placed before the court as proceedings rt authenticated by himself and his junior. One day, our man went to the regional head office of the A.C.B located in the district headquarters and obtained a copy of the proceedings of the operation to prepare himself for cross examination in the court.

On the morning of the date of hearing in the court, our man and his junior reached the city and met the public prosecutor who was in charge of the case on behalf of A.C.B in his chambers at the court. The public prosecutor was not cordial in his behavior towards our man and was issuing veiled warning to our man as though our man was about to commit a crime. The police officers of A.C.B who also came to the court from the town were not a happy lot. At about 12.00 noon the case of the S.I came for hearing and the name of our man was called. He entered the court hall and was made to stand while the culprit, the S.I, was sitting in a chair. Our man was asked by the judge all sundry questions about the exact location of the house of S. I and about tell tale marks around the house and also asked him to narrate the incidents that took place during the night of the raid in a rather brusque manner. The cross examination by the defense lawyer did give glimpse of the fate of the case a he was non-chalant in his approach and looked highly assured. At last the important evidence of the case ie., the sealed glass bottle of water which turned pink was produced before the court. Our man was dumb founded to see that the water in the glass bottle was transparent and colorless. After quite sometime, our man came to know that the case against the S.I was struck down. Lastly it was important to mention here that the A.C.B had borrowed a metal measuring tape from our man during the raid and they never bothered to return it again.

The atmosphere in the office was not congenial to the sincere, honest and un-compromising workers like our man when the work entrusted with was not individualistic like the designs of structures in which he had been involved so far. A finished product in the present unit was however the culmination of the efforts of several sub-units. The main object of this unit was to get prepared the finished product ie, detailed project reports of projects contemplated to be implemented as per pre-drawn programme and to send it to concerned authorities to get required clearances in order to prepare ground to put the project into execution. But in spite of its pivotal position, no importance is given to the unit and it generally acted as a rubber stamp. Hence, no importance was also given while selecting the staff to be posted to this unit. One can therefore imagine the quality of staff and their commitment to work. Nevertheless, the first two years of service went on smoothly. Gradually the sincere, hardworking and knowledgeable officers at the middle level and at the upper crest have been either retired or promoted to be posted elsewhere. The influx into these posts was below par and the middle level had no qualms in manipulating things to suit their ends. At the lower levels, except two or three officers, no one had any inkling of the job at hand and was neither intelligent nor knowledgeable and had no qualms either in manipulating things.

The general elections to the state legislative assembly were approaching. In that scenario, the idiot that he was, our man revealed his secret to one of his colleagues who was intelligent and hard working but was highly orthodox and deeply religious who still had no qualms in manipulating things as the situation demanded.

Hence, it was not difficult to imagine the travails and trauma he would be undergoing during the next three years in service after which he was due to retire. However, this time, our man tried to analyze and understand the methodology behind the working of these unnatural forces.

CHAPTER 7

2002-2004

Before going further, a look at our man in its entirety would be taken. At the fag end of his service, he had become so perfect in accomplishing the Jobs entrusted to him that the works of his colleagues and subordinates as well those of his superiors looked mundane to him. As already indicated; he had to scrutinize and finalize the reports based on the feeds from various channels. He used to find fault with the basics of each and every report to the displeasure of the staff, particularly his subordinates and colleagues, who developed an animosity towards him. He was further alienated from them because of his inappropriate admission that it took him ten years to complete his graduation and that he was never interested in the studies during that period. Another reason for his alienation was that he was not articulate and refined like them. The fact that he looked naïve and was aloof by nature had further estranged him.

The authorities were not interested in intellectualism in work. They wanted to push through the works. Hence, they were more interested in persons who obeyed them unflinchingly and who carried out miscellaneous works that were also important to run a public organization. Our man became abrasive and started criticizing the staff. Gradually he began to feel that he was a lowly man. He became impulsive. One day he revealed his past history to the orthodox gentleman, one of his two friends in the office, to impress upon him that he was a great man. After this narration, the gentleman kept himself distancing away from our man. Our man had become so frustrated that, one day, he telephoned his immediate superior officer and told to behave himself and threatened with dire consequences if he did not mend his ways. That was the start of another saga of his Journey into the unknown.

It all started with a mild head-ache which became severe within a span of forty eight hours. He now realized that he had come into the clutches of cosmic-forces. He also realized that not only he but some of the staff members connected to him in one way or other were also affected. But the degree of severity was more for him. He tried to be as humble as possible in those circumstances. But his humbleness was considered by the staff as a cause of his dubious actions resulting into the puzzling ill effects on their health in spasms. He also realized being humble alone did not provide solution to his problems, and unfavourable surroundings did not help him to overcome his affliction. He constantly altered his thinking process and strived hard to be positive in his thinking process which also did not yield any positive results. Surprisingly, in spite of severe and nerve wrenching pain which sometimes envelopes his whole head and un-ceasing absurd thoughts overtaking his mind, he was able to fully concentrate on his Job when needed and used to finish his Job impeccably.

In course of time, the affliction was only limited to our man. Insincere, dishonest and cunning persons were whole and hearty. It appeared to him that cunningness and complete submission before there cosmic forces being the only escaping route. He came to the conclusion that the modus operandi of these forces are beyond any rationale and did not distinguish between good and bad. Distancing himself away from unfavorable surroundings and taking recourse to medication did help him to overcome this affliction over a long period of time.

It is interesting to note certain observations he made during this period of affliction. Sometimes, his face wore a mask of serenity and pleasantness which he was always instantly aware of even without looking at the mirror in spite of intense turbulence in his mind. In general in may be said that serene and pleasant appearance can deceive human being and that the thoughts of such a face need not always be rational & pious. One day while he was sitting in his office, he suddenly felt that tranquility and sublimity enveloped his mind and body and that his mind was travelling into unknown unearthly spaces. At that moment, a woman appeared from nowhere and started cleaning the area. At same moment, a trace of pride germinated in his mind. All of a sudden, all that state of tranquility and sublimity disappeared. There is no place for pride in spiritualism. Smoking drinking and martial affairs etc are not immoral before God and are not a deterrent to achieve goals in spirituality. Only honesty, sincerity and humility do help. The cosmic forces are evil in nature and await the slightest chance to torment. The cosmic faces would destroy an individual until unless he was firm in his beliefs and actions irrespective of the nature of their objectives and rationale behind them.

Only after his retirement did the staff realizes the impeccable and outstanding nature of work he accomplished in this office.

The gamut of the conclusions he arrived at is discussed in the following chapters.

CHAPTER 8

Creator, God & Religion

Every object and particle in the world and universe have desires. Nothing in this universe exists without desire. The stars have desire to shine. The black holes have desire to draw and squeeze everything into their abdomens. The universe has desire to expand. The animals, plants and other creatures have desire to grow and to live. The human has basic desires i.e., to satiate hunger and sexual urge and to live. The various inert objects have their own kinds of desires. The least desirous being the inert and dull stones which have only one desire i.e., to bind themselves. The most desirous being the nature itself, which nurtures astounding bounties to the humanity, which brings both bloom and gloom. The human being thus naturally is also bestowed with plenty of desires that grew both in diversity and intensity in pace with the blossoming of his intelligence and un-raveling of nature's bounties with the passage of time. Even through security of common man has increased gradually with the passage of time with the evolution of intelligence and rational thinking, the weak and meek are still subdued. The less intelligent & weak have been exploited all through the history of mankind. The human is easily attracted to evil than to good. That might be the reason that the laws have been framed for society so that the evil might be contained as far as possible. The perceiving of evil may differ from one society to another. But it can be emphasized that evil is more dynamic then good in an abstract way. Why it is so?

Here it is to be pointed out that nothing in the world and the universe can either be perished or created absolutely out of nothing.

The desires also have not come out of nothing. They exist in the creation in the form of cosmic forces which pervade the entire universe. Where from these forces hence come? The Big Bang theory might be taken to recourse to explain the phenomena with a slight modification. That is that a dynamic and an immensely powerful object of infinite strength with plenty of desires contacted a static object of equally infinite strength but of minimum desires causing the big bang. The forces thus generated naturally have all the characteristics of these objects which mingled together and spread into the space in all directions into infinite, the evil forces being more dynamic then good forces. Here bad or evil is defined as having plenty of desires and good or pious having minimum of desires.

As already stated soul is nothing but knowledge & God is further evolution of soul. Then it can be said god is embodiment of knowledge. God is distinguished from Creator. God is limited to earth as God is evolution of man. Hence, God is a miniscule of the universe and cannot term as embodiment of all knowledge & hence he is part & parcel of creation. The definition that God is omnipotent, omniscient, omnipresent, equitable and magnanimous to all can be applied neither to God nor to the Creator in its entirety. If God is further evolution of soul, there may be several gods from whom a leader may have been elected. If not, then the most knowledgeable soul may be God. Then also, there may be replacements to the throne of God from time to time with the evolution of knowledge. As no knowledge of human being at any given time can be treated as perfect so is of God. No one including God can understand the dynamics and mechanism of cosmic forces.

The saints and seers are nothing but revelations of God who is not perfect in knowledge himself. Even though, every saint and seer without exception had basically preached good values and worked for the betterment of the human, their followers vitiated their sayings by forming religions which have transgressed into basic freedom of humans and have been based on narrow minded principles specially in respect of one gender of humans. This has been so because they could not comprehend precisely, clearly and impartially the good and bad values in each and every sphere of life. The religions are steeped in old age sayings and dogmas and irrational to a modern human. Most of the religions as on today have no place in the modern society. Even though the modern human in general believes in God, most of them do not follow religious scriptures. Liberty and freedom of expression and thought are the most important aspects for the evolution of human race for which the impediments being the religions in some societies. It is no denying the fact that where religions play pivotal role, the development of societies in several spheres of life is not encouraging.

An example is the part of the world in which our man lives. This is a peculiar and typical part of the world. Peculiar in the sense that even though the society is deeply divided, fragmented and fractured with an inward feeling of derisiveness towards each other, life still goes on smoothly as though there exists none. Typical in the sense that a vast majority of the people follow a religion which has no typical bearings of a religion in an universally accepted sense about which vast majority of them know nothing about, but still are bound together by this religious entity simple because of the mythological stories and religious festivals. This country which boasts of one of the earliest civilizations, unwittingly without being aware of the consequences that might follow, had divided the people into various categories based on the work they were entrusted with which later on has become their sole occupation for lively hood with no opportunities to make inroads into other avenues of works. The then religious seers legitimized this division of people and made an order of hierarchy classifying some groups of people superior to certain other groups who were termed as lowly and categorizing the rest of the groups as untouchables by decreeing that god created people thus. The cascading effect of this religious dogma is that majority of the people who had been termed lowly were oppressed for centuries and remain poor till today.

CHAPTER 9

Human & Society

Human race at an early part of its life was more instinctive than intelligent like other creatures. But, one thing that distinguishes human from others is rationale. Because of the capacity to think logically, the intelligence has gradually increased which in turn has increased the degree of rationalization. With the gradual increase in intelligence and there by rational thinking, new activities have come to encompass his life. From where and how this rationalization took seeds into his mind which is unheard of in other creatures? If the theory of gradual evolution is taken into account, rationale cannot be seeded into humans all of a sudden. But is it so? The nature surrounding us has astounding properties in its every element that follow precise and perfect laws which is only possible when its creator is rational of the highest order which is still beyond the imagination of human race. The creators have lost their entity as one being and hence desired to create specifically physically bound entities. It took about 200 millions years to evolve creatures of the present genre and the human to come into existence 500,000 years ago but it took 300,000 years for modern human to emerge. It is amazing to note that rationalism did not take seeds into animals even after their emergence 59 millions year ago. But the rationale of humans has gone to amazing heights just in 500,000 years of its existence, the pace being rapid in the last 100 years. The only reason might be that cosmic forces were not happy with the evolution of animals with limited application of limbs and intelligence and a creature of their liking could not be evolved form animals. They therefore created human being and injected rationalism into his brain which can only be sudden. The universe and earth has evolved gradually into objects of astounding beauty and admiration which can be only admired by humans. So, the man is created. The sad aspect of the rational of humans is that it comes from cosmic forces whose evil desires are more vibrant then good desires. Hence, the rationale can be dangerously two edged weapon.

The degree of freedom and extent of education enjoyed by human from time to time determine the degree of development, and security of human race. The crave for freedom of humans culminated in establishing democracies in most of the counties, even though the shackles of religion impede the growth of human spirit in certain regions. But absolute freedom as we are aware of gives rise to uninhibited exploitation of the weak and naive. As such, laws and regulations are framed to govern the society. Exploitation of people still takes place even in developed countries though in a limited way. But in other countries exploitation takes place in wide spheres of life and in large proportions. Still, democratic institutions try to address the problem of weaker sections as the political institutions are elected by the people whose majority consists of week in every country. Literacy and education of people can mitigate the exploitation. Until unless, the ruling classes governing the society or not selfish and power hungry, the laws of the land cannot be implemented in to-to. Education may also bring forth devious ways to fool the public who are also full of desires though inhibited.

One bad person can make ten bad persons easily. But one good person cannot make ten good persons so easily. Education may alone not bring-forth sanity and rationale. More education and there by more intelligence may twist the rationale to suite one's own ends. That is what is happening at least in this part of the world.

Knowledge is soul. That knowledge can be pure and chaste or otherwise. The more selfish and desirous a human becomes, the more the evolution of bad souls. The souls when liberated from human cannot be in general detached form the world with which they are accustomed to. They are always drawn to the world again through the process of rebirth. It hence may be concluded that humans of undesirable attitudes may go on multiplying until unless checked. Even, otherwise a few undesirable elements in important positions in society may vitiate the entire society if there are not checked. Selfishness arising out of plenty of desires may be the order of the day in the society. Religions in one way or other tried to stem the rot in their own way. Religious scriptures were based on the sociality and the accepted values of the then society and intellectual capacity of the then religious heads. As the time progressed, the man's crave for more freedom and rationale have increased making the religious scriptures redundant, which were considered so sacred as not to be altered. Most of the humans believe in God and religious festivals are performed in all their fervor. But the fundamental sayings of religions are not followed.

At least in this region it is observed that the humans pray God and perform rituals with the intention of getting his blessing in the form of physical benefits.

The human race should realize that their frailties are due to their father i.e., cosmic forces. And hence should not be ashamed of them. Otherwise, the humans have been endowed with astounding characteristics like intelligence, and rationale of very high order and amazing flexibility. The human race has conquered many extremities of nature and liberates himself from most of the genetically transmitted diseases and also those transmitted by nature. Similarly, man can conquer their frailties and weaknesses by making it a habit. Habit is such infectious that it can be cultivated for either good or bad. Once a man is habituated to lead a certain way of life, it is difficult to deter him to break away from the path. The most important and basic habit that the desires inculcate in humans is lying. If lying is minimized most of the undesirable desires, including pride will vanish thereby undermining the evil. A man in general who is forced to lead a life that is law abiding and truth full to society will be habituated to lead such a life without any difficulty. The important aspect being laws which should be rational and which should give as much freedom as possible to its citizens to pursue their activities in all spheres of life within the ambit of a secure society.

Finally, it is to be emphasized anything in excess as we know undermines the nature, the body and mind of human and the society. Excessiveness in high proportions destroys. Similarly excessive misuse of intelligence of high order will bring forth calamity to the human race. A day may come when the thought process of a human is transmitted to the fellow human.